A.K. GRAYSON is a Professor in the Department of Near Eastern Studies at the University of Toronto.

Early Assyriologists were lured to Babylonian studies by the light which cuneiform texts shed on ancient history and the Bible, and for later scholars this is still the attraction. The Age of Discovery is not past, and one can still read literature that has been unseen by the eyes of man for millennia. There are myriads of tablets lying in the ancient ruins of Iraq, Iran, Syria, and Turkey, waiting for the excavator's spade; in museums there are quantities of inscriptions that have not yet been made public.

Babylonian Historical-Literary Texts deals with such a group of inscriptions, which are in the British Museum and belong to a type of literature which has hitherto been very little known. The cuneiform text fragments are copied, transliterated, and translated. The outlook of the authors of the texts and the two literary genres to which the texts belong are analysed, and the significance of the late date of the tablets is discussed. A new study of the genre 'Akkadian prophecy' and a discussion of the Akkadian historical epic are also included. Of special interest among the text fragments are the Dynastic prophecy and the description of the coronation ceremony of the first Chaldaean king in the Nabopolassar epic.

TORONTO SEMITIC TEXTS AND STUDIES

Babylonian Historical-Literary Texts

A.K. GRAYSON

UNIVERSITY OF TORONTO PRESS
TORONTO AND BUFFALO

TORONTO SEMITIC TEXTS AND STUDIES

edited by J.W. Wevers and D.B. Redford

1

Essays on the Ancient Semitic World

2

Studies on the Ancient Palestinian World

3

Babylonian Historical-Literary Texts

A.K. GRAYSON

Toronto and Buffalo
Printed in Canada

Library of Congress Cataloging in Publication Data

Grayson, Albert Kirk.

Babylonian historical-literary texts.

(Toronto Semitic texts and studies; 3 ISSN 0082-5123)

Includes index.

1. Assyro-Babylonian literature–History and criticism.
2. Assyro-Babylonian literature.
3. Assyro-Babylonian language–Texts. I. Title.

PJ3671.G7 892',1 74-80888

ISBN 0-8020-5315-7

To
W.G. Lambert

Contents

Editors' Note

The Department of Near Eastern Studies of the University of Toronto on occasion presents through the series Toronto Semitic Texts and Studies papers of importance to the understanding of the Ancient Near East. These in general reflect the varied interests and fields represented by its members, and may represent linguistic, textual, historical or archaeological themes spanning the ancient world from Egypt to Iran. But in each instance some new facet, whether it be an unpublished text, some new interpretation of text or artifact or some new synthesis of known materials, is presented in the expectation that it will shed some light on the mysterious east.

In this volume we offer a number of new texts from Babylonia. Professor Grayson once again illustrates the truth of the old adage that the most rewarding archaeological discoveries may often be made in libraries and museums. The texts here presented were 'discovered' in the British Museum, and we are indebted to Professor Grayson for not waiting until he could present a definitive text and translation. Many interpretations are only provisional and will undoubtedly occasion heated discussions and learned debates among Assyriologists.

These texts will be of interest, however, to a much wider audience than cuneiform specialists. Historians will welcome the new light shed on Mesopotamian history through the examples of Historical Epic here presented. Students of Hebrew and Greek Apocalyptic Literature will welcome in particular Professor Grayson's presentation of a new example of the literary genre of Dynastic Prophecy. Students of literature will recognize in these texts universals of human nature which characterize all literature however exotic and dead their parent cultures may seem to a modern reader.

J.W. Wevers
D.B. Redford

Preface

Early Assyriologists were lured to Babylonian studies by the light that cuneiform texts shed upon ancient history and the Bible. To later scholars this is still the attraction; the Age of Discovery is not past. Today there are myriads of tablets lying in the ancient ruins of Iraq, Iran, Syria, and Turkey waiting for the excavator's spade. Even in museums there are vast quantities of inscriptions which have not yet been made public. For those who enjoy reading literature unseen by the eyes of man for millennia there remains a fertile field in Assyriology. The literary compositions published in this volume are an illustration of this, for they are presented to the public for the first time. The tablets on which they are inscribed belong to the British Museum and I am indebted to the trustees of that institution for permission to publish them.

The type of literature, historical-literary, which these compositions represent is poorly known and little studied. I have, therefore, included in this book a study of all the material together with special studies of the two genres to which the new texts belong. In chapter 1 there is an analysis of the outlook of the authors of these texts and of the literary genres. In addition, since the new tablets are from Persian or Seleucid Babylonia, I have discussed the special significance of their late date. In part I, chapter 2 presents a new study of the genre 'Akkadian prophecy' occasioned by the first publication of the Dynastic prophecy, which is treated in chapter 3. Note that this new text represents an important stage in the development of ancient Near Eastern apocalyptic literature. In part II I have grappled with the problem of the nature of the Akkadian historical epic, with specific reference to the Babylonian historical epic (chapter 4). The reason is the first publication (chapters 5–9) of considerable textual material for this genre. In part III (chapter 10) will be found several fragments of Babylonian historical-literary texts which cannot be precisely identified.

The texts have been edited in the usual manner of Assyriological publications and hand copies of them are provided.* Although I have spent many years studying, copying, and collating these inscriptions, the readings and interpretations offered here are still of a preliminary nature. It is always difficult to understand and appreciate the literature of a civilization different from one's own. This is even more the case when the temporal and geographic gaps are vast and when the literature is preserved in a fragmentary form, as in this case. There will, in the course of time, be many improvements on this initial effort. But it is high time these texts were made available to all.

There are a number of colleagues who have advised and encouraged me along the way. The generous co-operation of the staff of the Department of Western Asiatic Antiquities at the British Museum, particularly Dr R.D. Barnett, Dr E. Sollberger, and Mr C.B.F. Walker, deserves first mention in my acknowledgments. Professor W.G. Lambert, who introduced me to Akkadian literature almost two decades ago, has read and critized the manuscript in two drafts. I express my gratitude by dedicating this volume to him.

Professors R. Borger, J. Van Seters, and J.W. Wevers have each read the manuscript and suggested improvements for which I am most thankful. I also wish to thank Professor D.B. Redford, who assisted me with the Egyptian material, and Professor E. Reiner, who helped me with some textual problems. A special note of thanks

* In general the system of transliteration followed in this book is that followed by the Chicago Assyrian Dictionary. But when an ideogram appears in the cuneiform text the corresponding Akkadian form has been reconstructed wherever possible. When there is more than one ideogram for a word or proper name diacritical marks have been used to distinguish them. The system of diacritics outlined by W. von Soden and W. Röllig, Das Akkadische Syllabar (2nd ed.), Analecta Orientalia 42 (Rome 1967) pp. 75–6, has been used. In cases where only one ideogram is used for a particular word or name the ideogram has, for the reader's convenience, sometimes been added in parentheses. This is an arbitrary practice and not entirely consistent. The ideograms are, of course, listed under the relevant words in CAD and AHW. In the transliterations Akkadian has been italicized and in the translations uncertain renderings into English have also been italicized.

The dates quoted in this book follow J.A. Brinkman. See his chart in A.L. Oppenheim, Ancient Mesopotamia (Chicago 1964) pp.335–52. For late Kassite kings see his modifications in BIOR 27 (1970) p. 307, and for Post-Kassite kings of Babylonia and their Assyrian contemporaries see his chart in PKB plate II (after p. 76).

Since Late Babylonian grammatical forms are not familiar to very many Assyriologists I have frequently commented upon them and referred to relevant grammatical studies.

is due to Professor A. Pietersma, who guided me in the difficult area of the Sibylline oracles; the translation of the extract from that text in chapter 2 is his.

K. Hecker's Untersuchungen zur akkadischen Epik, AOATS 8 (1974), arrived after my manuscript was finished. Hecker has provided us with the first full study of the Akkadian epic and the reader will find it an extremely valuable reference work. Hecker does not devote much space to what I call the 'historical epic,' primarily because he did not have the material published in my book, and our two studies are to that extent complementary.

My thanks are due to the Canada Council for financial assistance which enabled me to collate the original tablets in the British Museum. Publication of this book has been made possible by a grant from the Humanities Research Council of Canada, using funds provided by the Canada Council, and a grant to the University of Toronto Press from the Andrew W. Mellon Foundation.

Toronto, October 1974

Abbreviations

AfO	Archiv für Orientforschung
AHW	W. von Soden, Akkadisches Handwörterbuch
ANET³	J.B. Pritchard (ed.), Ancient Near Eastern Texts Relating to the Old Testament, 3rd edition (Princeton 1969)
AnSt	Anatolian Studies
AOAT	Alter Orient und Altes Testament
BiOr	Bibliotheca Orientalis
Borger, HKL	R. Borger, Handbuch der Keilschriftliteratur I (Berlin 1967)
Brinkman, PKB	J.A. Brinkman, A Political History of Post-Kassite Babylonia, Analecta Orientalia 43 (Rome 1968)
CAD	The Assyrian Dictionary of the University of Chicago (Glückstadt/Chicago 1956–)
CT	Cuneiform Texts from Babylonian Tablets in the British Museum
GAG	W. von Soden, Grundriss der akkadischen Grammatik, Analecta Orientalia 33 (Rome 1952) and Ergänzungsheft zum GAG, Analecta Orientalia 47 (Rome 1969)
Grayson, ABC	A.K. Grayson, Assyrian and Babylonian Chronicles, Texts from Cuneiform Sources 5 (Glückstadt/Locust Valley 1975)
IEJ	Israel Exploration Journal
JCS	Journal of Cuneiform Studies
JNES	Journal of Near Eastern Studies
Lambert, BWL	W.G. Lambert, Babylonian Wisdom Literature (Oxford 1960)
Langdon, VAB 4	S. Langdon, Die neubabylonischen Königsinschriften, Vorderasiatische Bibliothek 4 (Leipzig 1912)
LBAT	T.G. Pinches and J.N. Strassmaier (ed. by A.J. Sachs), Late Babylonian Astronomical and Related Texts, Brown University Studies 18 (Providence 1955)
Or.n.s.	Orientalia nova series

RLA	E. Ebeling, B. Meissner, et al., Reallexikon der Assyriologie
Smith, BHT	S. Smith, Babylonian Historical Texts Relating to the Capture and Downfall of Babylon (London 1924)
STT	O.R. Gurney, J.J. Finkelstein, and P. Hulin, The Sultantepe Tablets (London 1957–64)
UF	Ugarit-Forschungen
VT	Vetus Testamentum
Weissbach, VAB3	F.H. Weissbach, Die Keilinschriften der Achämeniden, Vorderasiatische Bibliothek 3 (Leipzig 1911)
ZA	Zeitschrift für Assyriologie

NOTE ON TABLET SIGNATURES

Tablets given a registration date (e.g. 80-11-12, 3) are in the British Museum. The following are also signatures of British Museum tablets:

BM	British Museum
K	Kouyunjik
Rm	Rassam
sm	Smith
sp	Spartoli

BABYLONIAN HISTORICAL-LITERARY TEXTS

1

General Introduction

OUTLOOK OF THE AUTHORS

In the exclamation of the nobles at the coronation of Nabopolassar (chapter 7) lies the quintessence of the authors' view of the 'good life':

> O lord, O king, may you live forever!
> [May you conquer] the land of [your] enemies!
> May the king of the gods, Marduk, rejoice in you!

Here is a clear manifestation that the world of the authors of the Babylonian historical-literary texts revolved around Babylonia, its god, and its king; the best one could expect from life was a long, peaceful reign by a pious king. This ideal was never questioned or doubted. Not for them were the misgivings of the Job-like hero in the Babylonian 'I Will Praise the Lord of Wisdom' or the cynicism of the master and servant in the Babylonian 'Dialogue of Pessimism.' If bad things happened there was a reason and this reason always had its roots in impiety. It was a simple philosophy clothed in an elementary logic. It was the belief shared by the majority of ancient Babylonians. They, like mediaeval Europeans, looked to palace and church for guidance and security; if things went wrong at those lofty heights woe would ensue. Small wonder, then, that the activities of the king and his dealings with his gods are the focal point in the Babylonian historical-literary texts.

Another basic concept of these writers concerns the nature of the relationship between heavenly and earthly affairs. In the ancient Mesopotamian's view, natural and supernatural matters were tightly interwoven. Any disruption among the gods had its immediate effect upon earth for the gods constantly moved in both celestial and mundane spheres. Each god had one or more specific areas of activity and these were delineated by *šīmātu*, a term we usually translate as 'fates' or 'destinies.' Within his designated area or areas any god could act freely. Thus the god Ea was responsible for clever deeds and was called upon whenever cunning was required. Shamash, the sun god and supreme judge, was invoked whenever justice was in question. All events on earth had their origin in and were controlled by heavenly powers. Causation, the bogey of modern historiographers, was no problem to the ancient Mesopotamian; all things were ordered by the gods. Moreover, the gods normally announced their intentions in advance. Events were preceded by portents which man could learn not only to observe but to interpret correctly. The art of divining the future was one of hoary antiquity in Mesopotamia and produced highly trained groups of diviners and voluminous reference works. The belief that any event could be predicted if only one were sufficiently skilled to interpret the signs was as much a part of the minds of the authors of the historical-literary texts as the view that the gods caused everything and that the ideal good was a long, secure, and pious reign.

To the ancient Babylonians, past, present, and future were all part of one continuous stream of events in heaven and earth. There was indeed a beginning in the distant past, but there was no middle or end. Gods and men continued ad infinitum. There is thus no evidence in Babylonian thought of any eschatology nor is there any place for a cyclical view of history.[1] In fact, there was no word for 'history' in their language. Nevertheless they were fascinated by this eternal phenomenon and so enshrined their past for posterity in both prose and poetry.

A DESCRIPTION OF THE LITERARY GENRES[2]

There was no classification 'historical-literary' known to the ancient Mesopotamian scribe. This is a purely modern idea. They did ar-

1 See chapter 2, n. 34.

2 The more notable surveys of Assyrian and Babylonian literature are: O. Weber, Die Literatur der Babylonier und Assyrer (Leipzig 1907); B. Meissner, Die babylonisch-assyrische Literatur (Potsdam 1928); E. Dhorme, La Littérature babylonienne et assyrienne (Paris 1937); von Soden, 'Das Problem der zeitlichen Einordnung akkadischer Literaturwerke' in Mitteilungen der deutschen Orient-Gesellschaft 85 (1953) pp. 14–26; A. Falkenstein and W. von Soden, Sumerische und Akkadische Hymnen und Gebete (Zurich/Stuttgart 1953) pp. 7–56; Lambert, 'The Development of Thought and Literature in Ancient Mesopotamia' in BWL pp. 1–20; Hallo, 'New Viewpoints on Cuneiform Literature' in IEJ 12 (1962) pp. 13–26; Falkenstein, 'Die altorientalische Literatur' in W. von Einsiedel (ed.), Die Literaturen der Welt in ihrer mündlichen und schriftlichen Überlieferung (Zurich 1964) pp. 1–30. A useful bibliography is L.L. Orlin, Ancient Near Eastern Literature (Ann Arbor, Michigan 1969) and in particular note his comments on p. 31.

range literary works in 'series.' Long works which extended beyond the space available on one tablet were written on a series of tablets and at the end of each tablet was inscribed a colophon. The colophon usually contained, among other things, the number of the tablet, the title of the series, and the first few words of the next tablet. Thus the Gilgamesh epic, in a late recension, is arranged in twelve tablets; Enuma Elish in seven; and, since 'literary' in this respect can be taken to include all written materials of lasting value, there are series of lexical texts, omen texts, medical texts, etc. The grouping of texts into series has nothing to do with genre, for a series, in some cases, might also include compositions of quite different types. Thus the texts needed by the *kalû* priest in performing his duties were arranged in a series and included rituals, hymns, incantations, and omens.[3]

But the absence of a formal recognition of genre does not mean that the scribes were unaware of this higher order of classification; the fact is that they produced literary compositions exhibiting distinctive features of one or another genre. This is only natural, particularly in a society as conservative as the Mesopotamian. A scribe who wrote a 'new' work would of course be influenced by those literary compositions he already knew. No one writes, paints, sculpts, or composes in a vacuum. But the ancient writer was not as explicitly conscious of genre forms as we would be, so that the borders between differing genres may be hazy and often overlap. The modern scholar must avoid making sharper distinctions than the materials allow. In brief, the ancient Mesopotamian scribe consciously arranged literature according to series for essentially practical reasons but a more abstract classification according to genre is implicitly apparent.

The historical-literary category is, then, a modern term. But the texts I include under this heading have basic features in common; they belong to various refined literary forms and their content is concerned mainly with historical or natural events rather than with mythological or supernatural occurrences. Within this general category the modern scholar can discern three basic genres; prophecy, historical epic, and pseudo-autobiography.[4] As far as indigenous categorization of the texts in question is concerned,

3 Ancient catalogues of literary works do not seem to represent categorizations of literature in a formal sense.

4 Regarding the classification see the pioneering work of Güterbock, 'Die historische Tradition und ihre literarische Gestaltung bei Babyloniern und Hethitern bis 1200' in ZA 42 (1934) pp. 1–91; 44 (1938) pp. 45–149. Additions to this study are found in AfO 13 (1939–41) pp. 49–51.

there is clear evidence of one series, the Marduk and Shulgi prophetic speeches (see chapter 2). There is, in addition, the possibility that some of the Babylonian historical epics belonged to a series (see chapter 4).

Of the three genres of historical-literary texts only two, prophecy and historical epic, are treated in detail in this book since the new texts fall into these two areas. Nonetheless a discussion of all three genres, by way of general introduction, might well be appropriate at this point.[5]

An Akkadian prophecy is a prose composition consisting in the main of a number of 'predictions' of past events. It then concludes either with a 'prediction' of phenomena in the writer's day or with a genuine attempt to forecast future events. The author, in other words, uses vaticinia ex eventu to establish his credibility and then proceeds to his real purpose, which might be to justify a current idea or institution or, as it appears in the Dynastic prophecy, to forecast future doom for a hated enemy. There is some evidence that the

5 It should be noted that it was the practice to copy royal inscriptions, and copies were even kept of royal correspondence of special significance. The former requires no documentation. But the copying of royal correspondence is not as well known: for the Sumerian material see Jacobsen, JCS 7 (1953) pp. 39–42; Kraus, AfO 20 (1963) p. 153; and Kramer, ANET³ pp. 480-1. The practice is also attested in Akkadian. See A.K. Grayson, Assyrian Royal Inscriptions 1 (Wiesbaden 1972) §§888–96, 934–8 for a bibliography, commentary, and translation of four such letters. Possibly related, and certainly of interest, is the late Babylonian text in letter form published by Wiseman, Bulletin of the School of Oriental and African Studies 30 (1967) pp. 495–504; and the letter of Gilgamesh published by O.R. Gurney, STT 1, nos. 40–2; Proceedings of the British Academy 1955, pp. 37–8; and AnSt 7 (1957), pp. 127–36.

Previously published miscellaneous historiographical works have been discussed in Grayson, ABC pp. 2–4 and nn. 21–5. Regarding the composition from the reign of Nebuchadnezzar II called 'Nebuchadnezzar King of Justice' cf. Lambert, Iraq 27 (1965) pp. 1–11 and cf. chapter 4, n. 14. The fragment K 9952 published by Lambert, BWL pl. 12 and pp. 296–7 (cf. Grayson, ABC p. 57 and n. 58), may be an epic fragment but too little is preserved to be certain just where it belongs among historiographical works. The 'Kedorlaomer Texts' (cf. Grayson, ABC p. 57 and n. 63) pose special problems which necessitate a completely new study. To the bibliography in Borger, HKL p. 396 add: Brinkman, PKB pp. 80–2 and 361 (b); Astour in A. Altmann (ed.), Biblical Motifs, Philip W. Lown Institute of Advanced Judaic Studies, Brandeis University Studies and Texts 3 (1966) pp. 65–111 (in this study there are some doubtful interpretations of personal names in the cuneiform texts and the important observation of Landsberger [see chapter 4, n. 11] has not been taken into consideration [see further Emerton, VT 21 (1971). pp. 38–47]; Stokholm, 'Zur Überlieferung von Heliodor, Kuturnaḫḫunte und anderen missglückten Tempelräubern' in Studia Theologica 22 (1968) pp. 1–28. A further fragment of interest is known from a Pinches's copy and published by Walker in CT 51, no. 73.

genre has its roots in Sumerian literature. In the Hebrew scriptures parts of the Book of Daniel are strikingly similar to the form and rationale of Akkadian prophecy. Comparative material is also known from Egypt in the form of the admonitions of Ipu-Wer and the prophecy of Neferti.[6] The publication in this book of a previously unknown text of this type, the Dynastic prophecy, has significance both for the understanding of the intellectual climate of the early Hellenistic period in Babylonia and for the appreciation of the evolution of ancient Near Eastern apocalyptic literature. This has necessitated a completely new discussion of the genre in chapter 2.

Akkadian historical epics are poetic narratives concerned with the activities of kings. In contrast to other Akkadian epics the events described are essentially historical rather than mythological. There are both Assyrian and Babylonian historical epics. Assyrian historical epics, of which little has been preserved, have as their main theme the prowess of the king. Babylonian historical epics emphasize the supreme power of the god Marduk. The historical epic seems to be a genre restricted solely to Akkadian literature in the Ancient Near East for there are no comparable compositions in Sumerian, Hebrew, Egyptian,[7] or Hittite.[8] Very little Babylonian historical epic material was previously known but the texts in this book firmly establish the existence of the genre. Further details will be found in chapter 4.

Pseudo-autobiographies, sometimes called *narû*-literature, are first-person narrations by kings of their experiences.[9] The phenomena described are historical, legendary, and occasionally even supernatural in character. The best preserved composition is the

6 See Wilson, ANET[3] pp. 441–6 and 676. Further see the Demotic Chronicle in E. Bresciani and S. Donadoni, Litteratura e poesia dell'Antico Egitto (Turin 1969) pp. 551–60 (reference courtesy of R. Borger) and cf. Borger, BiOr 28 (1971) p. 23b.

7 Two Egyptian texts that might be comparable are the narratives of Penta-Wer and Inaros. For the first see A.H. Gardiner, The Kadesh Inscriptions of Ramesses II (Oxford 1960), and for the second see E. Bresciani, Der Kampf um den Panzer der Inaros (Vienna 1964). The crucial question is whether or not they are in poetry.

8 For fragments of the Hittite version of the King of Battle Epic (see Grayson, ABC p. 57, n. 60 for references to the Akkadian material) see the bibliography in E. Laroche, Catalogue des textes hittites (Paris 1971) p. 53, no. 310. The text published by Güterbock in ZA 44 (1938) pp. 101–45 is mythological in character.

9 See Güterbock, ZA 42 (1934) pp. 19–21; Gurney, AnSt 5 (1955) p. 93; Finkelstein, JCS 15 (1961) p. 101; Grayson and Lambert, JCS 18 (1964) p. 8; Borger, BiOr 28 (1971) p. 21 and n. 1; Grayson, ABC pp. 2–3. Güterbock described this material as '*narû*-literatur' but, since this leads to confusion with genuine royal inscriptions inscribed on *narû*, another designation is required.

Cuthaean legend of Naram-Sin, the central theme of which is that a king must heed the diviners or suffer dire consequences.[10] It is probably correct to assume that the other representatives of this genre were also didactic in intent.[11] The literary form originates in

10 For the Cuthaean legend see Gurney, STT 1, no. 30, and AnSt 5 (1955) pp. 93–113 and 6 (1956) pp. 163-4. (cf. von Soden, ZA 50 [1952] p. 180). An Old Babylonian version was published by Finkelstein, JCS 11 (1957) pp. 83–8 (cf. Pettinato, Or.n.s. 37 [1968] p. 194). For the Hittite version see Güterbock, ZA 44 (1938) pp. 49–67 and Hoffner, JCS 23 (1970) pp. 17–22. Also note the prism, inscribed in Akkadian, found at Boghazköi and published by Otten, AfO 22 (1968–9) p. 112 and Keilschrifttexte aus Boghazköi 19, no. 98. This appears to be yet another exemplar of the Cuthaean legend.

11 The other texts attested for this genre are:
a/ The Sargon birth legend: K 3401 + SM 2118, K 4470, BM 47449 were published by King CT 13, 42–3. K 7249 was published by Lambert CT 46, no. 46. It should be noted that BM 47449 is a fragment of a practice tablet: on the obverse appear remains of four columns of a lexical list; on the reverse appear the remains of four columns, some lexical, but one column consisting of the lines copied by King (CT 13, 43) which duplicate the Sargon birth legend; since a line is drawn after KÁ-*ia ip-ḫi* and there is then a blank space before the text breaks off, it appears that the scribe copied only this much of the birth legend (cf. Pinches, Proceedings of the Society of Biblical Archaeology 18 [1896] p. 256). The legend, excluding K 7249, was edited by L.W. King, Chronicles Concerning Early Babylonian Kings 2 (London 1907) pp. 87–96, and Güterbock, ZA 42 (1934) pp. 62–5. For older references see C. Bezold, Catalogue of the Cuneiform Tablets in the Kouyunjik Collection (London 1889–99) p. 529. Translations have been presented by Ebeling in H. Gressmann (ed.), Altorientalische Texte zum alten Testament (2nd ed. Berlin/Leipzig 1926) pp. 234–5, and Speiser (revised by Grayson), ANET[3] p. 119. Concerning the motif of the birth legend see Zimmern, Christusmythe p. 26; Jensen, RLA 1, pp. 322–4; and Redford, Numen 14 (1967) pp. 209–28.
b/ Another Sargon autobiography: MLC 641 was published by A.T. Clay, Babylonian Records in the Library of J. Pierpont Morgan 4 (New Haven 1923) no. 4. Cf. A.T. Clay, Amurru (Philadelphia 1909) p. 194; Güterbock, ZA 42, p. 64, n. 3; and Hirsch, AfO 20 (1963) p. 6.
c/ An autobiography of the Isin II dynasty: K 2660 was originally published by Smith in H.C. Rawlinson, The Cuneiform Inscriptions of Western Asia 3 (London 1870) 38, no. 2 and edited by H. Winckler, Altorientalische Forschungen 1 (Leipzig 1893–7) pp. 534–8. See now the edition of Tadmor, JNES 17 (1958) pp. 137–9. Also cf. Brinkman, PKB pp. 79–80, p. 106, and nn. 571 and 575. Note that this is a Middle Assyrian tablet of the type attributed to the library of Tiglath-pileser I (cf. Weidner, AfO 16 [1952–3] p. 203).
d/ An autobiography of the Kassite period: K 2599 + 3069 and K 10724 were published by Lambert, CT 46, nos. 49 and 50.

Two further texts which might be pseudo-autobiographies are: a Naram-Sin text ('BM Text') to be published by Sollberger and Grayson in a forthcoming volume of Revue d'Assyriologie; and the 'Sin of Sargon' text published by Tadmor, Eretz-Israel 5 (1958), pp. 150–62 and 93*. Two texts which definitely do not belong are the Naram-Sin text ('Geneva and Mari Tablets') edited by Sollberger and Grayson in the aforementioned article; and the prophetic speech of Marduk which is discussed in chapter 2.

the Sumerian period. No examples of such texts are known in Hebrew or Hittite[12] but a composition about Djoser in Egyptian is similar in form.[13]

DATE OF COMPOSITION

All of the tablets published in this book are from the period of Persian or Seleucid control of Babylonia and they probably all come from the city of Babylon. Although not all were originally composed in this late era, the fact that scribes were busy copying as well as creating this particular kind of literature is of interest. It shows that scholarship and creativity flourished in at least some scribal circles. Moreover, this activity reflects an atmosphere of regional pride possibly mixed with hatred towards foreign overlords. The copying and perhaps even the creation of epics, whose central theme was the Babylonian king and his relation to his gods and that in a time when there was no native monarch, is quite possibly more than just an attempt to preserve ancient traditions for posterity; it could well be an expression of rivalry with the Persian or Greek conquerors.[14] There may even have been strong resentment against the new masters, if my analysis of the Dynastic prophecy is correct. These tablets not only confirm the fact that Babylonian tradition was still strong in the Persian and Seleucid periods; they are also indicative of a strong sense of regional pride with, possibly, an element of anti-Hellenism. The whole question of anti-Hellenistic ferment in Babylonia will be dealt with in chapter 2.

In conclusion, something must be said about the literary merits of these works. Aesthetically the most attractive compositions to my mind are the historical epics. If they were better preserved they would be a pleasure to read. However it must be confessed they do not rival the artistic genius inherent in the Gilgamesh epic. The pseudo-autobiographies and the prophecies seem to me to be much lower down the scale of literary achievement. The texts within both groups are important and even have a creative spark, but in form and style they are far too stereotyped to be called great literature.

12 For a Hittite version of the Cuthaean legend of Naram-Sin see n. 11 above. The literary form of the Hittite text published by Güterbock in ZA 44 (1938) pp. 66–80 (also see E. Laroche, Catalogue des textes hittites [Paris 1971] p. 53, no. 311) is uncertain. Güterbock has suggested it is a free version of a royal inscription.

13 See Wilson, ANET[3] pp. 31–2.

14 One might also see this sense of rivalry in the history of Berossos and in legends about ancient Mesopotamians, such as Semiramis, preserved in Greek. Cf. chapter 2, n. 29d.

PART I AKKADIAN PROPHECIES

2

Introduction

Akkadian prophecies are actually pseudo-prophecies, for they consist in the main of predictions after the event (vaticinia ex eventu).[1] The predictions are divided according to reigns and often begin with some such phrase as 'a prince will arise.' Although the kings are never named it is sometimes possible to identify them on the basis of details provided in the 'prophetic' description.[2] The reigns are characterized as 'good' or 'bad' and the phraseology is borrowed from omen literature.[3]

Akkadian prophecies are to be distinguished from Akkadian oracles. Oracles, as the name indicates, were oral in origin although they might be preserved in a literary form. There is no evidence of an oral background to Akkadian prophecies. The two are also distinct in that, while an Akkadian prophecy described extensive periods of time in relatively vague terms, an oracle was a single divine utterance, usually through a named medium (although direct oracular communication through dreams is also attested) to a named individual, normally a king, and was related to a specific event and time. The oracle is attested in the Old Babylonian, Neo-

1 For previous discussions of the genre see Grayson and Lambert, JCS 18 (1964) pp. 7–30, and the bibliography of older literature on p. 7. Also note Hallo, IEJ 16 (1966) pp. 231–42; Biggs, Iraq 29 (1967) pp. 117–32; Lambert, Or.n.s. 39 (1970) pp. 175–7; Borger, BiOr 28 (1971) pp. 3–24.

2 This is particularly true in texts where regnal years are given. As will be shown in chapter 3, the regnal years in the Dynastic prophecy are of great assistance in dating the descriptions since they are actual numbers. The figures in Text A should, therefore, also be close to reality (see nn. 30 and 31 below). Regnal years do not appear in the Uruk prophecy nor in the Marduk and Shulgi prophetic speeches. Note that the events are fairly accurately described in the Dynastic prophecy and in the Marduk and Shulgi prophetic speeches and one should not be overly sceptical of the historical reliability of these texts.

3 More specifically it comes from omen apodoses. In addition some Akkadian prophecies are written with an abundance of ideograms typical of omen literature. The Dynastic prophecy and the Uruk prophecy, on the other hand, contain relatively few ideograms.

Assyrian, and early Hellenistic periods.[4] Akkadian prophecies are also quite different from Biblical prophecy.[5]

Thanks to the research of various scholars in recent years it has become reasonably clear which texts can properly be called Akkadian prophecies and which cannot. There are now five main compositions attested for this genre: the Dynastic prophecy (published here for the first time), Text A,[6] the Uruk prophecy,[7] the Marduk

4 For a recent translation of the Mari letters in which the oracles are reported see Moran, ANET[3] pp. 623–5, 629–32, and the bibliography there. Discussions of particular importance are W. von Soden, Die Welt des Orients 1 (1947–52) pp. 397–403; Malamat, Supplements to VT 15 (1966) pp. 207–27, Eretz-Israel 4 (1956) pp. 74–84 and 5 (1958) pp. 67–73; Huffmon, Biblical Archaeologist 31 (1968) pp. 101–24; Biggs, Iraq 29 (1967) p. 117, n. 4; and Moran, Biblica 50 (1969), pp. 15–56. Further oracle reports from Mari have been published by G. Dossin, Archives royales de Mari 10 (Paris 1967) (cf. W.H.Ph. Römer, Frauenbriefe, AOAT 12 [1971] pp. 18–29). An Old Babylonian oracle from Uruk has been translated by Biggs, ANET[3] p. 604. Oracles from the Neo-Assyrian period are attested for the reigns of Esarhaddon and Ashurbanipal.
Esarhaddon: J.A. Craig, Assyrian and Babylonian Religious Texts 1 (Leipzig 1895) nos. 22–5 (see Borger, HKL p. 67 for bibliography); S. Langdon, Tammuz and Ishtar (Oxford 1914) pls. 2–4 (see Borger, HKL p. 294 for bibliography); Pinches in H.C. Rawlinson, The Cuneiform Inscriptions of Western Asia 4 (2nd ed. London 1891) pl. 61 (see Borger, HKL p. 405 for bibliography and add Biggs, ANET[3] p. 605 and Weippert, Zeitschrift für die alttestamentliche Wissenschaft 84 [1972] pp. 473–4).
Ashurbanipal: Craig, Religious Texts 1, nos. 26–7 (see Borger, HKL p. 67 for bibliography); Leeper, CT 35, 13–15, 26–7, 30 (see Borger, HKL p. 298 for bibliography); and an oracle incorporated into a royal inscription (see Biggs, ANET[3] p. 606 for a translation and bibliography).

For an oracle report of the Neo-Assyrian period see Moran, ANET[3] pp. 625–6. For oracular dreams see A.L. Oppenheim, The Interpretation of Dreams in the Ancient Near East, Transactions of the American Philosophical Society N.S. 46/III (Philadelphia 1956). Also see Oppenheim, Ancient Mesopotamia (Chicago 1964) pp. 221–2. No native sources for Babylonian oracles of the Hellenistic period are known but references are made in Classical sources to 'Chaldaean' oracles. See Diodorus Sic. xvii 112:2–6 and xix 55:5–8; Arrian, Anabasis vii 16:5–17:6 and 22:1; and Plutarch, Alexander lxxiii 1–3.

5 For the contrast with Biblical prophecy see Hallo, IEJ 16 (1966) pp. 233–4.

6 See Grayson and Lambert, JCS 18 (1964) pp. 12–16 for an edition and note the translation by Biggs, ANET[3] pp. 606–7. The nomenclature 'Texts A, B, C, D' is from the article by Grayson and Lambert.

7 The Uruk prophecy was published by H. Hunger in XXVI/XXVII. vorläufiger Bericht über die von dem Deutschen Archäologischen Institut ... unternommenen Ausgrabungen in Uruk-Warka (Berlin 1972) p. 87 and pl. 25. I am grateful to Dr Hunger for sending me a transliteration of the text in advance of publication.

prophetic speech, and the Shulgi prophetic speech.[8] All of these works exhibit the basic characteristics already described.[9] It is necessary to make a sub-categorization of these documents, with the Dynastic prophecy, Text A, and the Uruk prophecy in one group and the Marduk and Shulgi prophetic speeches in another. The texts in the first group are in the third person while the prophetic speeches are in the form of an address in the first person. Despite this difference the five texts are closely related in form, style, and rationale.

On the other hand it has become obvious that certain compositions which have hitherto been called Akkadian prophecies do not belong to this genre.[10] These are Text B and LBAT 1543. Text B[11] differs in having a mythological introduction[12] and in its connections with astrological literature.[13] LBAT 1543, to which attention was drawn by Biggs,[14] has astrological features different from Text B and the format of the content is quite distinct.[15]

There is no longer any reason to suppose that, apart from phraseology, there is a connection between Akkadian prophecies and omen literature. With the establishment of the text of the

8 Thanks to Borger's keen observation these two texts, the Marduk and Shulgi prophetic speeches, have now been properly pieced together. See Borger, BiOr 28 (1971) pp. 3–24 for editions. Note that Text C belongs to the Shulgi prophetic speech and Text D to the Marduk prophetic speech. Although the similarity of the Marduk text to the Akkadian prophecies had been noted previously (see JCS 18 [1964] p. 8) it is now clear that it is better classified, together with the Shulgi text, as 'prophecy' rather than 'pseudo-autobiography.' Cf. Borger, BiOr 28 (1971) p. 21.

9 It is of interest that the Marduk and Shulgi prophetic speeches belong to one series.

10 Cf. Lambert, Or.n.s. 39 (1970) pp. 176–7 and Borger, BiOr 28 (1971) p. 23.

11 For the latest edition (including new fragments) see Biggs, Iraq 29 (1967) pp. 120–8.

12 Cf. ibid. p. 118 and n. 9 and ANET[3] p. 606. There is no need to assume that Text A first side i 1–8 is a 'mythological' introduction.

13 This is now clear from the new fragments identified by Biggs (q.v. for comment). It is noteworthy that at least five examplars of Text B are attested.

14 Biggs, Iraq 29 (1967) pp. 128–132.

15 The beginning of each section is unfortunately broken, but since the end of the first line in each section describes the death of the ruler (and the astrological omen connected with it), the line could hardly begin 'a prince will arise.' The remainder of each section seems to be concerned with the successor's rule. The use of regnal years in both Text B and LBAT 1543 is different from that in the prophecies (see n. 2 above). 'Seven years' in line 24 of Text B is purely literary and the same comment can be applied to the 'twenty-seven' and 'seven' in LBAT 1543. Indeed, no such sequence of regnal years is attested in Babylonian chronography.

Marduk and Shulgi prophetic speeches and the publication of the Dynastic prophecy it is now clear, as I emphasized some time ago,[16] that the relation of the prophecies (and the Fürstenspiegel) to divination is purely stylistic. What could be more natural for the authors of these texts than to draw upon their extensive scribal education in omen literature (prognostic texts make up the single largest category in Ashurbanipal's library)[17] for their 'predictions'?[18]

But what was the purpose of the Akkadian prophecies? Thanks to Borger's work, there is now no doubt that the Marduk prophetic speech was written during the reign of Nebuchadnezzar I (c. 1126–1105 B.C.) and was part of the momentous religious movement of the time, the elevation of the god Marduk to kingship over the gods.[19] By means of vaticinia ex eventu the author intended to show that this great event had been predicted centuries before. The purpose of the Shulgi prophetic speech, which appears after the Marduk prophetic speech in the same literary series in the library of Ashurbanipal, is not so easily ascertained since the text is badly broken, particularly towards the end. The speech concluded about the time of the fall of the Kassite dynasty or possibly as late as Nebuchadnezzar I.[20] The cities of Nippur and Babylon, and their inhabitants, have a prominent role in the composition and one wonders if the text was intended, like the Fürstenspiegel (which in addition was concerned with Sippar), to lend prophetic power to claims of these cities to privileged status in a period when these privileges were being challenged.[21] The Uruk prophecy was obviously written in an attempt to prove the great importance of the city of Uruk, though it is not certain when to date the events described.

As to the purpose of the Dynastic prophecy, two facts stand out:

16 Grayson, 'Divination and the Babylonian Chronicles' in La Divination en Mésopotamie ancienne; XIVe rencontre assyriologique internationale (Paris 1966), pp. 69–76. Also see Grayson, ABC p. 37.

17 See A.L. Oppenheim, Ancient Mesopotamia (Chicago 1964) p. 16.

18 Text B and LBAT 1543 have, on the other hand, a real if peculiar position in omen literature. Cf. Biggs Iraq 29 (1967) p. 117.

19 See Lambert 'The Reign of Nebuchadnezzar I: A Turning Point in the History of Ancient Mesopotamian Religion' in W.S. McCullough (ed.), The Seed of Wisdom: Essays in Honour of T.J. Meek (Toronto 1964) pp. 3–13.

20 I see no reason to assume that the fall of the Kassite dynasty was omitted. There is sufficient space for such a description in the lacuna at the end of column v and beginning of vi. Also v 16 does not necessarily represent the beginning of the 'real' prophecy. Cf. Borger, BiOr 28 (1971) p. 23.

21 For example, and this is mere speculation, could the city of Nippur, with the usurpation of Enlil's position in the pantheon by Marduk, be concerned to show that its traditional privileges were on a par with those of Babylon?

each of the first three columns contains a description of a change or fall of a dynasty (column i: fall of Assyria, rise of Babylonia; column ii: fall of Babylonia, rise of Persia; column iii: fall of Persia, rise of Macedonia); and each change results in the reign of the founder of the new dynasty being either 'good' or 'bad,' 'good' reigns alternating with 'bad' (the reigns at the end of columns i and iii are 'good'; the reign at the end of ii seems to be 'bad'). These facts suggest that the badly preserved column iv may have concerned the next change of dynasty, viz. the capture of Babylon by Seleucus I, and further that his reign may have been described as 'bad.'[22] If this was the case, then the Dynastic prophecy is a strong expression of anti-Seleucid sentiment.

Is there any other evidence for anti-Seleucid or anti-Hellenistic feeling in Babylonia? One looks in vain in cuneiform sources but there is a passage in Greek in the Sibylline oracles which may be relevant.[23] The prediction in question is found in book III, which is a large collection of predictions said to have been uttered by a Babylonian Sibyl.[24] The section in which this text appears constitutes a miscellaneous group of unrelated predictions against various cities and nations.[25] The relevant lines predict the Macedonian conquest

22 The tenuous nature of the evidence must be stressed. In the passage itself only the phrase 'will be extinguished' (iv 6) indicates that the reign is described as 'bad.' Otherwise the only evidence is the supposed pattern of the prophecy, i.e. that columns i and iii end with 'good' reigns while column ii ends with a 'bad' reign. This last point, the interpretation of the concluding description (ii 22–4) of Cyrus's reign, is not entirely certain. One could regard as descriptions of a 'good' reign at least two of the relevant lines, viz. ii 23 (cf. chapter 3, n. 10) and ii 24 (merely omit *ul* 'not' from the restoration). It is only in ii 22 (*eli māti idannin* 'he will oppress the land') that there is no room for ambiguity, particularly since the same phrase is found earlier (ii 14) in the midst of the description of the reign of Nabonidus as 'bad.'

23 For the Sibylline oracles see J. Geffcken, Die Oracula Sibyllina, Die griechischen christlichen Schriftsteller der ersten drei Jahrhunderte 8 (Leipzig 1902). Also see J. Geffcken, Komposition und Entstehungszeit der Oracula Sibyllina in Texte und Untersuchungen zur Geschichte der altchristlichen Literatur, Archiv für die von der Kirchenväter-Commission der Kgl. preussischen Akademie der Wissenschaften unternommene Ausgabe der älteren christlichen Schriftsteller, N.F. 8/1 (Leipzig 1902); H.N. Bate, The Sibylline Oracles, books 3–5 (London/New York 1918); A. Peretti, La Sibilla Babilonese nella propaganda Ellenistica (Florence 1943); A. Kurfess, Sibyllinische Weissagungen (Berlin 1951); V. Nikiprowetzky, La Troisième Sibylle (Paris 1970).

24 She was called Sabbe or Sambethe. See Nikiprowetzky, Sibylle pp. 12–14 for suggested etymologies. Pausanias x 12:9 and Ps. Justin, Cohortatio 37:7 say she was the daughter of Berossos.

25 III 295–488. Cf. Nikiprowetzky Sibylle pp. 67–8.

of Asia and Europe, the reconstruction of Babylon, and Macedonian collapse. Here is the text:

ἀλλὰ Μακηδονίη βαρὺ τέξεται Ἀσίδι πῆμα,
Εὐρώπῃ δὲ μέγιστον ἀνασταχυώσεται ἄγλος
ἐκ γενεῆς Κρονίδαο νόθων δούλων τε γενέθλης.
κείνη καὶ Βαβυλῶνα πόλιν δεδομήσετ' ἐρυμνήν,
καὶ πάσης ὁπόσην ἐπιδάρκεται ἠέλιος γῆν
δεσπότις αὐδηθεῖσα κακαῖς ἄτῃσιν ὀλεῖται
οὔνομ' ἐν ὀψιγόνοισι πολυπλάγκτοισιν ἔχουσα.[26]

Macedonia shall produce grievous woe for Asia,
And for Europe there shall shoot up great distress
From the race of the Kronid, a breed of bastards and slaves.
It shall rebuild even Babylon the fortified city,
And, though called mistress of every land
On which the sun shines, shall perish in dire follies,
Leaving [only] a name among far-wandering posterity.

It is possible that this text is Babylonian in origin and related to Akkadian prophecy. It is known that there are Babylonian elements in book III of the Sibylline oracles[27] and the specific reference to Babylon, the only city mentioned, in this prediction strongly suggests a Babylonian provenance. Furthermore, the form of the prediction is reminiscent of Akkadian prophecies.[28] Of particular importance is the anti-Macedonian sentiment of these lines. It is not at all impossible that this passage is a survival in Greek of a native Babylonian prophecy which had its origins in anti-Hellenistic feeling in Babylonia. As already suggested, the Dynastic prophecy may have arisen in a similar climate of opinion. It is, of course, quite conceivable that such a climate existed at a time when Babylon was overshadowed by the creation of Seleucia-on-the-Tigris. That disconsolate scribes would have used the prophetic form to express

26 III 381–7.

27 The traditional authorship suggests this. For discussion of the complex textual history see the bibliography cited in n. 24 above and for the recognition of Babylonian elements see Geffcken, Komposition pp. 3–5; P. Schnabel, Berossos (Leipzig/Berlin 1923) pp. 69–93; Kurfess, Weissagungen pp. 15–16; and Nikiprowetzky, Sibylle p. 15.

28 The vagueness of the prediction precludes 'oracle' in the strict sense outlined earlier in this chapter.

their hostility towards Hellenism is quite possible.[29] But a firm conclusion must await further evidence.

Unfortunately it is impossible to make any positive statement concerning the purpose of the fifth Akkadian prophecy, Text A,

29 A recent attempt to prove the existence of anti-Hellenistic feeling in Babylonia has not been very successful. S.K. Eddy in The King is Dead: Studies in the Near Eastern Resistance to Hellenism 334–31 B.C. (Lincoln, Nebraska 1961) pp. 101–32 and 156–62 has woven together scattered evidence from Greek and Akkadian sources. But note:
a/ Eddy's statement in The King is Dead pp. 115–16 and n. 31 that the fate of Seleucia-on-the-Tigris 'was frequently forecast in Chaldaean astrological tablets of the early Seleukid era' is based on a misunderstanding. See T.G. Pinches, The Old Testament in the Light of the Historical Records and Legends of Assyria and Babylonia (2nd ed. London 1903) pp. 476–8. The text (RM IV, 97) translated on these pages by Pinches is a late copy of an ancient lament. See Pinches, Proceedings of the Society of Biblical Archaeology 23 (1901) pp. 197–8 and the bibliography in Borger, HKL p. 400.
b/ There was strong Babylonian hostility towards Antigonus, as Eddy, The King is Dead pp. 112–13 notes. See the chronicle concerning the Diadochi r. 14–33 (Grayson, ABC Chronicle 10) for a description of the mistreatment of Babylonia by Antigonus. Antigonus was not called 'king' in this chronicle, in the Hellenistic king list (Sachs and Wiseman, Iraq 16 [1954] pp. 202–11 and cf. Grayson, *lišān mitḫurti*, AOAT 1 [1969] p. 106, n. 7), nor in dates on Babylonian documents (see R.A. Parker and W.H. Dubberstein, Babylonian Chronology 626 B.C.–A.D. 75, Brown University Studies 19 [Providence, 1956] p. 20). But he does appear (without title) in the Uruk king list and the Saros canon (see van Dijk, XVIII. vorläufiger Bericht über die von dem deutschen archäologischen Institut ... unternommenen Ausgrabungen in Uruk-Warka [Berlin 1962] pp. 58–9). (Cf. the attitude of some Babylonian chronographers towards Sennacherib, whom they refused to recognize after his destruction of Babylon [see Grayson, ABC appendix B, sub Sennacherib].) But hostility towards Antigonus does not mean hostility towards Hellenism.
c/ Eddy in The King is Dead p. 120 says, with reference to the reign of Antiochus I: 'The author of the [Babylonian] *Chronicle* grumbles that because of the scarcity of silver the unfamiliar "copper coins of Greece" must be used and that because the country has been stripped of wealth to support the army there is scabies in the land.' The text, which is an astronomical diary (BM 92688 + 92689 published by Smith, BHT no. 6) and therefore closely related to the Babylonian chronicle series, merely states these facts in the objective manner of a Babylonian chronicle; it does not 'grumble.' Similarly the famine and the selling of children, referred to by Eddy, are merely recorded. There is no complaint within the text itself.
d/ Although my knowledge of the Greek sources is limited I do not see that the material quoted by Eddy points unilaterally towards anti-Hellenism in Babylonia. Tales such as the Semiramis legend, in which Mesopotamian heroes are credited with deeds comparable to those of Alexander, do not in themselves prove passive resistance to Hellenism. At the most they are evidence of a sense of rivalry (cf. my comments under Date of Composition in chapter 1). Similarly Berossos's attempt to educate the Greeks in Babylonian history was hardly anti-Hellenic. The 'Chaldaean' oracles noted by Eddy concerned only Alexander and Antigonus. The

because of the badly broken state of the tablet.[30] By analogy with the Dynastic prophecy one might speculate that the fall or change of dynasties theme was the motif here as well.[31] Certainly it can be assumed that the author had some clearly tendentious theme, as did the authors of the other prophecies.

The relation of Akkadian prophecies to Jewish apocalyptic[32] was

---

Babylonian hatred for Antigonus has already been noted. But the oracles advising Alexander to enter Babylon by a different gate are not necessarily anti-Alexandrian. One could just as easily regard it as concern on the part of the Babylonian diviners that Alexander have the favour of the gods.

e/ Before leaving this critique, it is as well to note that the Hellenistic monarchs were patrons of Babylonian cults. The temple Esagil at Babylon was renovated during the time of Alexander the Great and apparently with his encouragement (see Grayson, ABC Chronicle 10 commentary to obverse 6 [and addenda]). Antiochus I restored Esagil and Ezida (see Weissbach, VAB 3 pp. 132–5 and Oppenheim, ANET^3 p. 317; Grayson, ABC Chronicle 11; and cf. Schnabel, Berossos [Leipzig/Berlin 1923] pp. 9–13) and apparently re-established the regular income of the temple Egishnugal at Ur (see Grayson, ABC Chronicle 11). Seleucus III provided offerings for the New Year's Festival at Babylon into which had been incorporated the royal cult (see Grayson, ABC addenda et corrigenda Chronicle 13b). Temple restoration at Uruk was undertaken during the reigns of Seleucus II (see Falkenstein, Topographie von Uruk [Leipzig 1941] pp. 4–5), Antiochus III (see ibid. pp. 6–7), and Antiochus IV (see Rostovtzeff, Seleucid Babylonia, Yale Classical Studies 3 [1932] pp. 6–7). Further cf. Grayson, ABC addenda et corrigenda n. 2.

f/ The view expressed by Widengren in A. Dietrich, G. Widengren, and F.M. Heichelheim, Orientalische Geschichte von Kyros bis Mohammed, Lieferung 2 (Leiden 1966) pp. 9–10 that Hellenization made some progress at Uruk but that eventually a reaction set in rests largely on the accidental discovery of a cache of literary texts in cuneiform at Seleucid Uruk, and on the fact that some men with Hellenistic names had sons with Semitic names.

30 See Grayson and Lambert, JCS 18 (1964) p. 9 for older suggestions on the identity of the reigns described. Hallo, IEJ 16 (1966) pp. 235–40, has recently proposed the latter reigns of the Isin II dynasty. Brinkman, PKB p. 129, n. 762 says there is as much against as for the proposal while Borger, BiOr 28 (1971) p. 23 thinks it is plausible.

31 This would fit Weidner's proposal in AfO 13 (1939–41) p. 236 that first side ii describes the reigns of the last four Kassite kings. If so, iii might describe the first two kings, or the first and last, of Isin II since 'eight years' would suit either Itti-Marduk-balatu or Nabu-shumu-libur. But it is difficult to make any proposal for second side ii. In any case, the whole matter of specific identification is moot and I am not urging either proposal over the other. As stated in our original article however (JCS 18 [1964] p. 9) Böhl's identification with the Sargonid period is improbable.

32 Regarding ancient near eastern apocalyptic in general see the discussion and bibliography by Hallo in IEJ 16 (1966) pp. 240–2. Also note Alexander, 'Medieval Apocalypses as Historical Sources' in American Historical Review 73 (1968) pp. 997–1018. Professor John Van Seters has suggested to me that the prediction in

recognized some time ago but the publication of the Dynastic prophecy now sheds startling new light on this relationship. As Lambert and I observed, and as Hallo corroborated,[33] there is similarity between the Babylonian genre and certain parts of the Book of Daniel (8: 23–5 and 11: 3–45). In style, form, and rationale there is a striking resemblance. The appearance of the Dynastic prophecy now adds significant evidence of this close connection. In the Dynastic prophecy the concept of the rise and fall of empires, which must have its roots in the dynastic tradition of Mesopotamian chronography, is mirrored by the similar concept in Daniel. Compare also the rubric regarding secrecy at the end of the Dynastic prophecy with the command in Daniel to keep the book sealed. But of prime significance is the possibility that the Dynastic prophecy concludes, as suggested both by internal evidence and on analogy with the prophecy in the Sibylline oracles, with a real attempt to predict the downfall of the Hellenistic kings.[34] The Marduk prophetic speech and probably the Shulgi prophetic speech conclude with vaticinia ex eventu in the 'prophet's' time. It is only in the Dynastic prophecy that there appears to be real prophecy at the end of a series of vaticinia ex eventu. A real attempt to predict, preceded by pseudo-predictions, is one of the salient features of apocalyptic. It

---

Genesis 15:13–16, which seems to contain an element of vaticinia ex eventu, is also similar. Cf. VT 22 (1972) p. 456.

33 See Grayson and Lambert, JCS 18 (1964) p. 10 and cf. HALLO, IEJ 16 (1966) pp. 240–2.

34 If my analysis of column iv of the Dynastic prophecy is correct (see n. 22 above), it ends with the prediction of the downfall of the Seleucids. It must be emphasized that there is no suggestion in any Akkadian prophecy of a climactic end to world history (see Lambert, Or.n.s. 39 [1970] pp. 176–7 and Borger, BiOr 28 [1971] p. 24). The opinion expressed by me in JCS 18 (1964) p. 10 that the Babylonians had a cyclical view of history must be disregarded. The underlying concept of divination does not, as I have come to realize through greater acquaintance with Babylonian omens, imply either a cyclical or deterministic view of history. Omens are nothing more than divine messages foretelling in a general way what the gods have decided to do. The gods themselves act freely. This view I presented in a paper entitled 'Clio in Cuneiform Costume: Assyro-Babylonian Ideas About History' to the Toronto Oriental Club on 6 February 1968. Also note Lambert's remarks in Or.n.s. 39 (1970) p. 175, n. 7, and Oudtestamentische Studien 17 (1972) pp. 70–1. It is against this background we must view the Akkadian prophecies. The general pattern of the Dynastic prophecy – alternating 'good' and 'bad' reigns at the end of each change of dynasty – is no proof of a cyclical view. It is merely a tendentious pattern designed to serve a specific purpose. It should not be regarded as the basic Babylonian view of all history. The alternating 'good' and 'bad' reigns in Text B are not relevant here because of the astrological nature of the text.

would appear, therefore, that the Dynastic prophecy reflects an important stage in the development of apocalyptic literature in the ancient Near East.[35]

The origin of the genre we call Akkadian prophecy is uncertain. The Marduk prophetic speech obviously dates from the reign of Nebuchadnezzar I and the Shulgi prophetic speech may be earlier. Whether the genre can be traced all the way back to Sumerian times remains to be proven.[36]

There are a number of fragments which may belong to the Akkadian prophecies or to omen literature. Particularly noteworthy is BM 34903, of which a copy by Pinches has been published by C.B.F. Walker as CT 51, no. 122. The traces are reminiscent of the Dynastic prophecy and it is not impossible that it came from the same tablet, although there is no join. K 3253 published in JCS 18 (1964), pp. 25 and 27 (and cf. p. 8a) is of special interest since it has phraseology similar to that of the Dynastic prophecy.[37] Three fragments noted in previous publications are K 4458, K 14372, and SM 1205.[38] Finally, note the fragment BM 52028 opposite.

To summarize: the identity of a specific genre which we call Akkadian prophecy is now reasonably well established. To date, five texts belonging to this category are known, Text A, the Dynastic prophecy, the Uruk prophecy, the Marduk prophetic speech, and the Shulgi prophetic speech. The rationale of the authors of the Akkadian prophecies was to prove their reliability as prophets by means of vaticinia ex eventu. Although there is no meaningful connection with omen literature there is a genuine relation with apocalyptic. The Dynastic prophecy, in particular, in its apparent attempt to predict future events, appears to mark a crucial step in the evolution of apocalyptic literature in the ancient Near East.

35 It is still not, however, apocalyptic in the strict sense of that word. In particular there are no eschatological features. See the able analysis of Hallo, IEJ 16 (1966) pp. 240–2. I think it best to maintain the general term 'prophecies' for these texts since the word does not necessarily imply Biblical prophecy. But the term 'apocalypses' does imply a very specific genre.

36 I am indebted to Professor J.J.A. van Dijk for a private communication that drew my attention to Sumerian material which may be related. Cf. Hallo, IEJ 16 (1966) p. 242, n. 79 and Lambert, Or.n.s. 39 (1970) p. 176, n. 3.

37 Line 1 = iii 20; 2a = ii 14, 22; 2b = iii 14.

38 See Grayson and Lambert, JCS 18 (1964) p. 8a. K 4458 was published by Weidner, AfO 13 (1939–41) p. 235. K 14372 and SM 1205 were published by Grayson and Lambert, JCS 18 (1964) pp. 25 and 27 (cf. p. 21a) respectively. For SM 1205 also see Borger, BiOr 28 (1971) p. 22, n. 7.

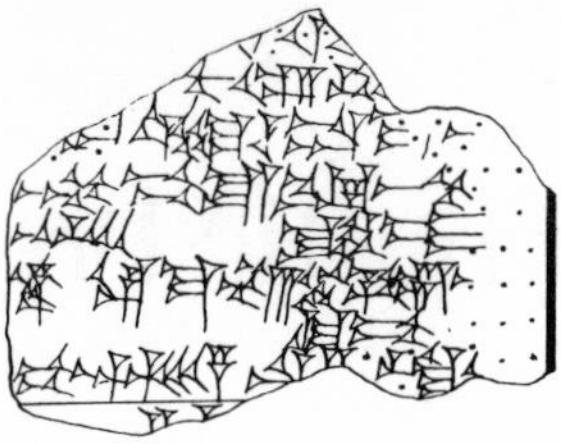

BM 52028 (82-3-23, 3062)

3

The Dynastic Prophecy

As indicated in the previous chapter the Dynastic prophecy is one of the most unusual and significant pieces of Babylonian literature to be published in many a decade. It is a description, in prophetic terms, of the rise and fall of dynasties or empires, including the fall of Assyria and rise of Babylonia, the fall of Babylonia and rise of Persia, the fall of Persia and the rise of the Hellenistic monarchies. Although as in other prophecies no names of kings are given, there are enough circumstantial details to identify the periods described.

The text is preserved on one broken tablet, BM 40623 (81–4–28, 168), although it is not impossible that BM 34903, published by Walker as CT 51, no. 122, is a fragment of the same tablet. The main tablet appears to have had an introductory section (i 1–6) of which only a few traces are preserved. After a horizontal line the first 'prophecy' appears (i 7–25). Although only the ends of lines are preserved, it is clear that this section contained a description of the fall of Assyria and the rise of the Chaldaean dynasty. This is indicated by the theme of the paragraph, destruction followed by reconstruction, and reference to the army of Assyria (i 10) and booty entering Babylon (i 20), as well as the fact that the fall of Babylon and the fall of Persia are the remaining two topics with which the 'prophet' is concerned. Also note the reference to Nippur (i 24) which calls to mind the important role played by this city in the Assyro-Babylonian conflict.[1] Finally the redecoration of Esagil (?) and Ezida (i 21) and the building of the palace at Babylon (i 23) suit admirably for the reign of Nabopolassar. The section concludes with the length-of-reign formula, from which the numeral is missing, and a horizontal line.

After a lacuna of indeterminate size the remains of another 'prophecy' appear (ii 1–10). Since the following section (ii 11–16) is clearly about Nabonidus, this paragraph must concern some period

1 See Grayson, ABC Chronicle 2:1 ff.

after the reign of Nabopolassar and before Nabonidus. Four kings reigned during this time – Nebuchadnezzar II (forty-three years), Evil-Merodach (two years), Neriglissar (three years and eight months) and Labashi-Marduk (three months).[2] The 'three years' of this paragraph (ii 6) must, therefore, refer to Neriglissar.[3] The son who succeeds him but who 'will not [*be master of the land*]' (ii 10) must refer to Labashi-Marduk.[4] This would fit reasonably with the pattern in column iii where the reigns of the last two members of the Achaemenid dynasty are described.

With the next section (ii 11–16) we enter a better preserved and highly significant portion of the composition. That this paragraph refers to Nabonidus is self-evident. In addition to the seventeen-year reign (ii 13), note the description of the king as 'a re[bel] prince' (ii 11) and as having established the 'dynasty of Harran' (ii 12). The general description of his 'bad' reign (ii 14–16) is reminiscent of the description of Nabonidus's reign in the Cyrus cylinder,[5] and the interruption of the Akitu festival, which is apparently mentioned in ii 14, calls to mind the Nabonidus chronicle and the Nabonidus verse account.[6]

The 'king of Elam' in the next 'prophecy' (ii 17–24) is clearly Cyrus[7] and the luckless king who lost his throne, Nabonidus. The 'prophecy' that the deposed king would be settled in another land (ii 19–21) supports the statement of Berossos[8] that Cyrus spared Nabonidus and made him governor of Carmania, though Xenophon says Nabonidus was killed.[9] In the next few lines (ii 22–4) a 'bad' reign is described and this passage seems still to refer to Cyrus.[10]

2 Uruk king list. See Grayson, ABC appendix D for bibliography.
3 Perhaps one should restore '(and) eight months' in the break.
4 Cf. the comment of Nabonidus on the incompetence of Labashi-Marduk in Langdon, VAB 4, p. 276 iv 34–42. For a recent discussion of this point see Beljawski in M. Lurker (ed.) In Memoriam E. Unger: Beiträge zu Geschichte, Kultur, und Religion des Alten Orients (Baden-Baden 1971) pp. 197 and 205–6.
5 See Weissbach, VAB 3, p. 2:5–9.
6 For the Nabonidus chronicle see Grayson, ABC Chronicle 7. For the Nabonidus verse account see Smith BHT no. 3.
7 Cf. Grayson, ABC Chronicle 7 (Nabonidus chronicle) iii 26 where Cambyses is apparently said to have worn 'Elamite' dress. The use of the term 'Elam' may be a deliberate archaism, as is the use of 'Hanaean' for Alexander in column iii.
8 Josephus, Contra Apionem i 20–1 and Eusebius, Evang. ix 41.
9 Xenophon, Cyropaedia VII v 29–33.
10 ii 23 is reminiscent of the Cyrus cylinder (Weissbach, VAB 3, p. 6) 28–30 but in the cylinder the event is cast in a favourable light.

It is difficult to decide where the description of Cyrus ends since the scribe temporarily abandons the practice of indicating the conclusion of a reign by drawing a horizontal line (a practice he consistently follows in columns i and iv and most of ii). Certainly another reign is referred to in iii 4 ('two years'). The most plausible division would be after ii 24 (the bottom of the column) with a new reign beginning in iii 1. This means that no length-of-reign formula has been given for Cyrus, a feature which is also absent for Alexander (see below).

It is evident from the events and the sequence of regnal years in column iii that the first section (iii 1–5) concerns Arses who ruled for two years before being assassinated by the eunuch-general Bagoas. For the same reasons there can be no doubt that iii 6–8 describe the five-year rule of Darius III, for whom Bagoas obtained the throne although Darius was not from the same branch of the Achaemenid line as Arses.

The context as well as internal clues strongly indicate that iii 9–23 describe the invasion of Asia by Alexander the Great. The term *Ḫanû*, which was originally the name of an Amorite tribe in the Old Babylonian period, is known from other late cuneiform contexts to refer to inhabitants of Thrace.[11] Its use here, rather than *Makkadunû*, with reference to the conqueror who had come by way of Thrace, reflects an archaizing tendency.[12] The defeat of the king in the first battle (iii 9–13) probably refers to the defeat of Darius's army at Issus (Granicus is less likely). After his defeat, the king reorganizes his troops and with the help of Babylonian deities (that Darius III could be assisted by Babylonian gods is not surprising – Marduk's aid to Cyrus is well attested in Babylonian sources)[13] brings about the defeat of the Hanaean! Both the syntax in iii 17 and the fact that the Babylonian gods were on the king's side make this clear (despite the apparent ambiguity of the third masculine singular suffix in this passage). The Hanaeans are plundered, the booty is brought into the king's palace, and a 'good' reign ensues. The problem, of course, is how to reconcile the defeat of the Hanaeans with historical fact – the victory of Alexander at Gaugamela! For this I have no answer. It is extremely unlikely that the 'prophet' would

11 See Grayson, ABC appendix C, s.v.

12 See n. 7 above.

13 Marduk and Sin caused Cyrus to defeat the Medes and capture Astyages (Langdon, VAB 4, pp. 218–20, i 18–33). Marduk also caused Cyrus to invade Babylonia and depose Nabonidus (see the Cyrus cylinder).

deliberately falsify the outcome and aftermath of such a famous and well-known battle.[14]

Traces of three further paragraphs appear on column iv (1–6) and it is noteworthy that all three paragraphs are short. The phrase 'seize the land' (iv 4) calls to mind Seleucus I and, if this is correct, the previous two sections would refer to Philip Arrhidaeus (iv 1–2) and Alexander IV (iv 3).

The remainder of the tablet contains two further sections. The first (iv 7–9) states that this text is a secret of the great gods which is to be shown only to the initiated. Statements of this kind are attested on many Babylonian tablets in the late period. The last section (iv 10–14) is the colophon.

The text is written by an experienced hand and is surprisingly free of errors.[15] The scribe's penchant for syllabic writings, an unusual feature for a prophecy, is noteworthy.[16] There is such a slight curvature to the fragment that it is difficult to decide how much is missing, although there is a real possibility that very little is broken away. The estimated breadth of columns ii and iii has been established on the basis of context and restorations made accordingly. Only in ii 18–22 is there some doubt and the square brackets are therefore enclosed in parentheses.

14 In the previous chapter it was observed that there appears to be an alternating pattern of 'good' and 'bad' reigns at the end of each 'fall' (and column). But this pattern would not demand Darius's victory. Alexander's reign could have been regarded as 'good.' It is unlikely that the defeat of the Hanaean is already part of a real prediction. The traces of column iv certainly seem to be describing three further reigns.

15 The same minor error occurs in ii 9 and 19. Note the erasures in ii 10, 15; iii 16.

16 Cf. chapter 2, n. 3.

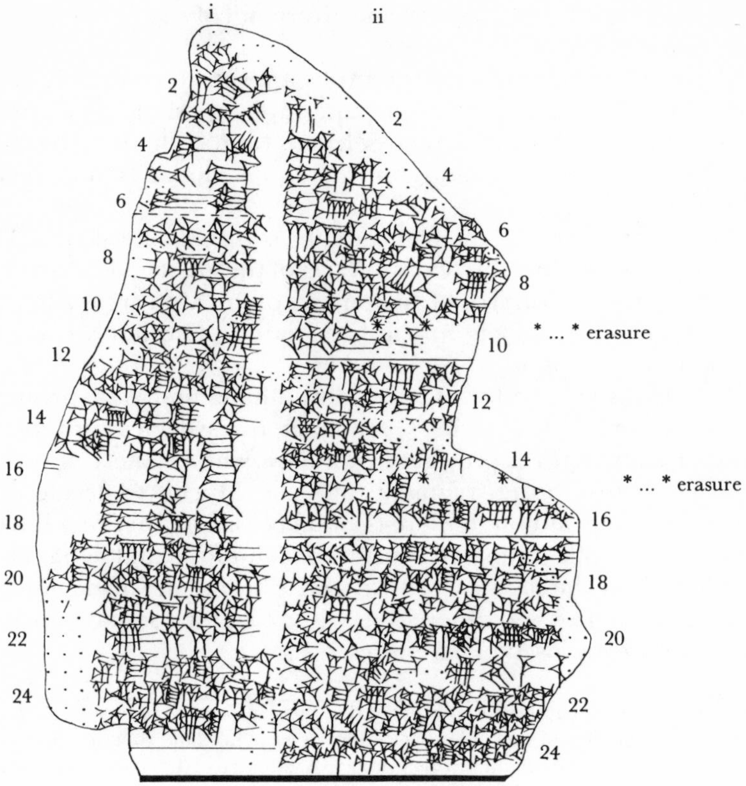

Obverse of BM 40623 (81-4-28, 168)

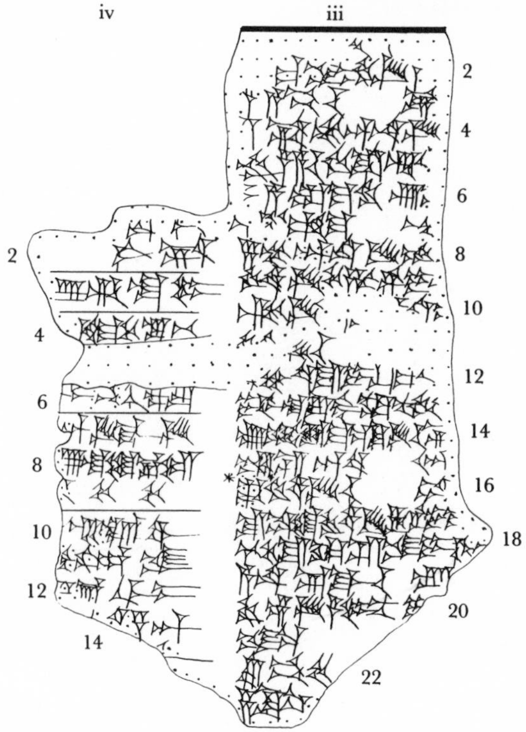

*... * written over erasure

Reverse of BM 40623 (81-4-28, 168)

TRANSLITERATION

i

Lacuna

1 [... ... *in-ni*(?)]-*in-n*[*i*]
2 [... ... *in*(?)]-*ni-in-ni*
3 [... ...] MU *e-zib*
4 [... ...] x GAL^{meš}
5 [... ...] NUMUN-*ma*
6 [... ...] x *i-mur*

— — — — — — — — — — — — — —

7 [... ...] *ár-kát* u_4-*mu*
8 [... ...] *is-sa-kip*
9 [... ... *i*]*g-gam-mar*
10 [... ... *e-mu*(?)]-*qu* ^{kur}*Aš-šur*^{ki}
11 [... ...] ŠEŠ(?) KÙ GA *ú*
12 [... ...] x *itebbâ*(zi)-*am-ma*
13 [... ...] *Bābili*^{ki} *itebbâ*(zi)-*am-ma*
14 [... ...] *is-sa-ak-ki-pi*
15 [... ...]-*nu-tu inašši*(íl)-*ma*
16 [... ...] x *illak*(gin)-*ma*
17 [... ...] *i-ṣab-bat*
18 [... ...] *i-naq-qar*
19 [... ...] *i-sa-am-ma-ak*
20 [... ... *šillatum*(?) *ka-bit*(?)]-*tum ana Bābili*^{ki} *ú-še-reb*
21 [... ... *É-sag-í*]*l*(?) *ù É-zi-da*
22 [... ...] *ú-za-a-an*
23 [... ...] *ekal Bābili*^{ki} *ippuš*^{uš}
24 [... ...] x *Nippur*(En.líl)^{ki} *a-na Bābili*^{ki}
25 [x^{ta} MU.A]N.NA^{meš} *šarru-ú-tu ippuš*^{uš}

---

i 1–6 It is possible that these lines are the remains of an introduction since verbs in i 3, 5 ([*i*(?)]-*zer-ma*), and 6 appear to be preterites rather than presents. Also the end of i 1 and 2 could be interpreted '[*which are un*]*alterable*' (the N of *enû* usually appears with the negative) and taken to refer to the predictions which follow. The end of i 3 might be 'he/I left [*for poste*]*rity*' ([*ana ṣât*/*arkât* u_4]-*mu e-zib* – cf. i 7) and the end of i 6 'he saw' (*īmur*).

TRANSLATION

i

Lacuna

1–6 Too broken for translation

7 [… …] later time
8 [… …] will be overthrown.
9 [… …] will come to an end.
10 [… … *ar*]*my* of Assyria
11 [… …] …
12 [… …] will attack and
13 [… …] Babylon, will attack and
14 [… …] will be overthrown.
15 [… …] he will bear … and
16 [… …] … he will come and
17 [… …] he will seize.
18 [… …] he will destroy.
19 [… …] he will …
20 [… …] he will bring [*exten*]*sive* [*booty*] into Babylon.
21 [… … *Esagi*]*l* and Ezida
22 [… …] he will decorate.
23 [… …] he will build the palace of Babylon.
24 [… …] … Nippur to Babylon
25 [for N year]s he will exercise sovereignty.

---

i 6f. There appears to be a horizontal line drawn between i 6 and 7.

i 8 *is-sa-kip*: Note *i-sa-ak-kip* in ii 5 and *is-sa-ak-ki-pi* in i 14. On the latter orthography see von Soden, GAG §18e and Gelb, BIOR 12 (1955), pp. 100–1.

i 20 Cf. iii 18f.

i 24 The sign before Nippur is neither TA nor TU (for *ul-tu*).

ii

Lacuna

1 x [... ...]
2 *a-a-*[... ...]
3 ta x [... ...]
4 *i-te-lu* x [... ...]
5 *i-sa-ak-kip* x [... ...]
6 III^{ta} MU.AN.NA^{meš} [*šarru-ú-tu ippuš*^{uš}]
7 *pal-lu-uk-ku ù* x [... ...]
8 *a-na nišē*^{meš}*-šú ú-k*[*a*(?)- ...]
9 *arki-šú mār-šú* ⟨*ina*⟩ *kússê u*[*š-ša-ab*(?) (...)]
10 *ul i-*(erasure)[*bêl*(?) *māta*(?)]

---

11 *ellâ*(e$_{11}$)^{a} ^{lú}*rubû ḫa-a*[*m-ma-'u* (...)]
12 *palê*^{e} *Ḫar-ra-an*^{k}[^{i} ...]
13 XVII^{ta} MU.[A]N.NA^{me}[^{š} *šarru-ú-tu ippuš*^{uš}]
14 *eli māti i-dan-nin-ma isinni*(?) *É*(?)*-sa*[*g*(?)*-íl*(?) ...]

15 *dūru ina Bābìli*^{ki} (erasure) x [...]
16 *lemut*(ḫul)*-tì a-na* ^{kur}*Akkadî*^{ki} *ú-ṣa-am-m*[*a-ar*]

---

17 *šàr* ^{kur}*Elamti*^{ki} *i-te-eb* ^{giš}*ḫaṭṭa* x x [x x]
18 *ina kússê-šú i-de-ek-ke-e-šu-ma* ([...])
19 *kússâ isabbat u šarru šá* ⟨*ina*⟩ *kússê* ZI⌜*ú*⌝ ([...])

20 *šàr* ^{kur}*Elamti*^{ki} *a-šar-šú ú-nak-k*[*a-ar* (...)]
21 *ina māti šá-nam-ma ú-še-šeb-šú* ([...])
22 *šarru šu-ú eli māti i-dan-nin-m*[*a* (...)]

23 *mātāti*(kur.kur)^{meš} *ka-la-ši-na bil-tum* x [...]
24 *i-na palê*^{e}*-šú* ^{kur}*Akkadî*^{ki} *šub-tum ni-i*[*ḫ-tum ul uššab*]

ii 2 Cf. iii 6.

ii 4 See the note to ii 17.

ii 7 Cf. *mukîn pal-lu-uk-ki šamê u erṣetim* Weissbach VAB 3, p. 134:15 (Antiochus I); *mukîn pu-lu-uk šamê u erṣetim* Langdon, VAB 4, p. 100 ii 23; and see von Soden, AHw p. 879a.

ii 10 Cf. Text A (JCS 18 [1964] p. 13) first side ii 19.

ii

Lacuna

1 ... [......]
2 ... [......]
3 ... [......]
4 *will go up from* [......]
5 will overthrow [......]
6 For three years [he will exercise sovereignty].
7 Borders and ... [......]
8 For his people he will [......]
9 After his (death) his son will [ascend] the throne ([...])
10 (But) he will not [*be master of the land*].

---

11 A re[bel] prince will arise ([...])
12 The dynasty of Harran [*he will establish*].
13 For seventeen years [he will exercise sovereignty].
14 He will oppress (lit. 'be stronger than') the land and the *festival* of *Esa*[*gil* he will *cancel*].
15 A fortress in Babylon [he will build].
16 He will plot evil against Akkad.

---

17 A king of Elam will arise, the sceptre ... [...]
18 He will remove him from his throne and ([...])
19 He will take the throne and the king who arose ⟨from⟩ the throne ([...])
20 The king of Elam will change his place ([...])
21 He will settle him in another land ([...])
22 That king will oppress (lit. 'be stronger than') the land an[d (...)]
23 All the lands [*will bring to him*] tribute.
24 During his reign Akkad [will not enjoy] a peaceful abode.

ii 14 *eli māti i-dan-nin-ma*: The same phrase occurs in ii 22. For *idannin* in other prophecies see JCS 18 (1964) p. 27, K 3253:2 and ibid. p. 21 r. i 4.
isinni(?) *É*(?)-*sa*[*g*(?)-*il*(?)]: The readings fit the traces. Cf. *i-sin-nu* ZAG.MUG *lu-šá-ab-ṭi-il* Smith, BHT pl. 6 ii 11 (Nabonidus verse account).

ii 17 The end of the line is difficult. The IB is certainly not LU (cf. ii 4).

ii 21 One expects *ina māti šanîtimma*.

ii 22 Cf. ii 14 and commentary.

iii

1 [...] x x [... ...]
2 x-[*b*]*a*/[*m*]*a-tum šarrāni*^{meš} x [... ...]
3 *šá a-bi-šú az*(?)-[... ...]
4 ⸢II⸣^{ta} MU.AN.NA^{meš} [*šarru-ú-tu ippuš*^{uš}]
5 *šarra šá-a-šú* ^{lú}*ša-re-š*[*i* ...]
6 ⸢*a*⸣-*a-um-ma* ^{lú}*rubû*⸢^{ú}⸣ [...]
7 ⸢*itebbâ*(zi)⸣ -*am-ma kús*[*sâ iṣabbat*]
8 V MU.AN.NA^{meš} *šarru*-[*ú-tu ippuš*^{uš}]
9 ^{lú}*ummāni*^{meš} ^{kur}*Ḫa-ni-i* x [...]
10 *itebbû*(zi)^{meš} x x x x x [...]
11 ⸢^{lú}*ummāni*^{meš}⸣-*šú* [... ...]
12 [*ḫ*]*u-bu-ut-su i-hab-ba-t*[*ú šil-lat-su*]
13 *i-šal-la-lu ár-ka-nu* ^{lú}*um*[*māni*^{meš}-*šú* (...)]
14 *ú-kaṣ-ṣar-ma* ^{giš}*kakkē*^{meš}-*šú in*[*aššì*(íl)]
15 ^{d}*En-líl* ^{d}*Šamaš u* ^{d}[*Marduk*(?)]
16 *idi*(da) ^{lu}*ummāni*^{meš}-*šú illakū*(gin)[^{meš}-*ma*]
17 *su-kup-tu* ^{lú}*ummāni*^{meš} *Ḫa-ni-i* ⸢*i*⸣-[*šak-ka-an*]

18 *šil-lat-su ka-bit-tum i-šal-l*[*a-al-ma*]
19 *a-na ekalli-šú ú*-[*še-reb*(?)]
20 ^{lú}*nišū*^{meš} *šá lum-nu i*-[*mu-ru*(?)]
21 *dum-qa* [*immarū*(?)]
22 *lìb-bi māti* [*iṭâb*(?)]
23 *za-ku-tú* [... ...]

Lacuna

iii 5 *ša rēši*: See Brinkman, PKB pp. 309–11 and 396.

iii 6 I am not certain what to restore at the end of this line. Cf. ii 11.

iii 14 Cf. JCS 18 (1964) p. 27, K 3253:2.

iii 15 For the restoration cf. Langdon, VAB 4, p. 68:25 (Nabopolassar) and p. 88, no. 9:3 (Nebuchadnezzar II).

iii

1 [...] ... [... ...]
2 ... kings ... [... ...]
3 Which/of his father ... [... ...]
4 For two years [he will exercise sovereignty].
5 A eunuch [*will murder*] that king.
6 *Any* prince [*will arise*],
7 will attack and [seize] the thr[one].
8 For five years [he will exercise] sovereignty.
9 The army of the Hanaeans [...]
10 will attack ... ... [...]
11 [*The Hanaeans will bring about the defeat of*] his army.
12–14 They will plunder and rob him. Afterwards he (the king) will refit [his] army and ra[ise] his weapons.

15 Enlil, Shamash, and [*Marduk*]
16 will go at the side of his army [and]
17 the overthrow of the army of the Hanaean he will [bring about].
18 He will carry off his extensive booty and
19 [*bring* (*it*)] into his palace.
20 The people who *had* [*experienced*] misfortune
21 [*will enjoy*] well-being.
22 The mood of the land [will be a happy one].
23 Tax exemption [... ...]
Lacuna

iii 19 Cf. i 20.

iii 20 Cf. *nišū*^{meš} *šá lum-na* I[GI] JCS 18 (1964) p. 27, K 3253:1 and Text A (ibid. p. 13) second side ii 14.

iii 22 Cf. Text A (ibid. p. 12) first side ii 3.

iv

Lacuna (about six lines)

1 [… …] x x

2 [x^{ta} MU.AN.NA^{meš} *šarru-ú-tu*(?)] *ippuš^{uš}*

---

3 [… …] *ú-d/tal-la-lu$_{4}$*

---

4 [… …]-*am-ma māta iṣabbat^{bat}*

5 [… …]

6 [… …] *i-bé-el-lu*

---

7 [… …] *ilāni*^{meš} *rabûti*^{meš}

8 [… … *la mu-du*]-*ú la tu-kal-lam*

9 [… … *b*]*ēl mātāti*(kur.kur)

---

10 [… …] x *iltēn^{en} tup-pi*

11 [… …] *mun-nab-tum*

12 [… …] *šá-ṭir bari*(igi.tab)

13 [… …] x šá an

14 [… …] x

Lacuna

iv 3 *ú-d/tal-la-lu$_{4}$*: There are several possibilities: D of *dalālu* – see CAD 3 (D), p. 178 and AHW p. 153 'They will oppress'; D of *talālu*(?) – see von Soden Or.n.s. 22 (1953), pp. 260–1 (?); Dt of *alālu* A – see CAD 1/1 (A), pp. 329–31 and AHW p. 34 'They will be suspended'; Dt of *elēlu* – see CAD 4 (E), pp. 80–3 and AHW pp. 197–8 'They will be purified.'

iv

Lacuna (about six lines)

1 [......] ...
2 [*For* N *years*] he will exercise [*sovereignty*].

---

3 [......] ...

---

4 [...... *will attack*] and seize the land.
5 [......]
6 [......] will be extinguished.

---

7 [...... a secret/taboo of] the great gods
8 [You may show it to the initiated but to the uninitiat]ed you must not show (it).
9 [It is a secret/taboo of Marduk, lo]rd of the lands.

---

10 [......] first, tablet
11 [......] Munnabtum
12 [......] written, collated
13 [......] ...
14 [......] ...

Lacuna

iv 7–9 For other examples of *Geheimwissen* see Borger, RLA 3, pp. 188–91 and Hunger, Babylonische und Assyrische Kolophone, AOAT 2 (1968) pp. 13–14. In particular note ibid. nos. 98 and 206.

iv 10 *iltēn tuppi*: These two words are in the wrong position in the colophon to be interpreted 'First tablet (of the series ...).'

iv 11 For Munnabtu as a personal name see von Soden, AHW p. 673b.

PART II BABYLONIAN HISTORICAL EPICS

4
Introduction

A study of Babylonian historical epics inevitably leads one into the whole realm of Babylonian literature, but more particularly to a consideration of the epic since it must be clear from the outset what relation there is between Babylonian epics and Babylonian historical epics.[1] If one considers the epic form simply as being a lengthy poetic narrative, then there are a number of Babylonian compositions which come under this heading. Some are purely mythological in character. Such are Enuma Elish, the myth of (An)Zu, and the myth of Nergal and Ereshkigal.[2] Others have a historical or legendary quality about them while also containing mythological material. These are the stories of Gilgamesh, Etana, Atra-hasis, Era, and Adapa.[3] A third group is concerned with historical heroes, and mythological themes are absent. These can be called historical epics.[4]

The texts about Babylonian kings published here are historical epics and possibly belong to one series. In addition to their formal similarity they are all known from late copies written by similar hands. Within the category of historical epic one should also include

1 For a bibliography of discussions of Babylonian literature see chapter 1, n. 2.

2 See Speiser and Grayson, 'Akkadian Myths and Epics' in ANET[3] pp. 60–119 and 501–18.

3 See ibid., and for the Era epic see L. Cagni, L'Epopea di Erra, Studi Semitici 34 (Rome 1969).

4 The tendency in comprehensive collections has been to place the groups together: cf. P. Jensen, Assyrisch-babylonische Mythen und Epen, Keilinschriftliche Bibliothek 6/1 (Berlin 1901); Ebeling, 'Mythen und Epen' in H. Gressmann (ed.) Altorientalische Texte zum alten Testament (2nd ed. Berlin/Leipzig 1926) pp. 108–240; Speiser and Grayson, ANET[3] pp. 60–119 and 501–18. Also cf. B. Meissner, 'Mythen und Epen' in Die babylonisch-assyrische Literatur (Potsdam 1928) pp. 42–52. On the other hand at least one scholar, E. Dhorme (La Littérature babylonienne et assyrienne [Paris 1937] pp. 35–72), has separated 'La Littérature mythologique' (pp. 35–50) from 'La Littérature épique' (pp. 51–72). (After completion of the manuscript the following came to the author's attention: Nougayrol, 'L'Épopée babylonienne' in Accademia Nazionale dei Lincei, Problemi attuali di scienza e di cultura, Quaderno N. 139 [Rome 1970] pp. 839–58.)

poetic narratives about Sargon,[5] Naram-Sin,[6] the fall of Ur,[7] Nebuchadnezzar I,[8] some Middle Assyrian kings,[9] and the siege of Uruk.[10] All of these texts are in Akkadian and thus, while the epic form is Sumerian in origin, the historical epic seems to have been an Akkadian phenomenon.

In this chapter we are concerned only with the Babylonian texts of this genre. Second-millennium kings are the subject of at least three Babylonian historical epics, all preserved in copies from the Late Babylonian period.[11] There are two epics about Kassite kings, Kurigalzu and Adad-shuma-usur. The main source for the Kurigalzu epic is, oddly enough, Chronicle P. This chronicle quotes extensively from an epic in its description of two battles fought by Kurigalzu. It is possible that the fragment in chapter 5, in which hostilities with Elam are also narrated, is part of the same epic (see that chapter for details). The other Kassite (see chapter 6) epic is about Adad-shuma-usur and is much better preserved. The third epic concerned with the second millennium is about Nebuchadnezzar I. Only the beginning of the text is available, preserved on a fragment from Kouyunjik, and here is narrated Nebuchadnezzar's lament over the absence of the god Marduk from Babylon. The epic must have gone on to describe Nebuchadnezzar's heroic campaign

5 King of Battle epic – see Grayson, ABC p. 57, n. 60 for bibliography.

6 The Naram-Sin epic is known only from a rough copy of Pinches (the location of the original tablet is unknown) published by Güterbock, AfO 13 (1939–41) pp. 46–9 and cf. von Soden, JNES 19 (1960) p. 164. Also note the comments of Grayson and Sollberger in an article to appear in a forthcoming issue of Revue d'Assyriologie.

7 Falkenstein, Literarische Keilschrifttexte aus Uruk (Berlin 1931) no. 43.

8 See below.

9 See Grayson, ABC p. 57 and nn. 64–6.

10 R.C. Thompson, The Epic of Gilgamesh (Oxford 1930) pl. 59 and see pp. 91–2 and Jensen, Keilinschriftliche Bibliothek 6/1 (Berlin 1901) pp. 272–3. In the portion preserved there is described the misery within Uruk during a three-year siege by an enemy which the goddess Ishtar will not oppose. One is reminded of the woe brought upon Uruk by the Sutaeans in the Era epic IV 52–62, where Ishtar is said to have brought the enemy against the city in her anger. Von Soden, UF 3 (1971) pp. 255–6 has plausibly suggested that this passage in the Era epic should be connected with the cultic disturbances known to have taken place in Uruk in the eighth century B.C. in the reigns of Eriba-Marduk (see Langdon, VAB 4, pp. 274–6, col. iii) and Nabu-nasir (see Brinkman, PKB p. 233).

11 It is also possible that K 9952 and at least one of the Kedorlaomer Texts, BM 34062 (SP 158 + SP II, 962) (cf. Landsberger [apud Güterbock], ZA 42 (1934) p. 21), are historical epic fragments about this period. See chapter 1, n.5.

to Elam and his victorious return to Babylon with Marduk's statue.[12]

The subject of the remaining historical epics is the Chaldaean dynasty; there is thus a hiatus of several centuries.[13] This material, all published here for the first time, consists of three fragments. The first is a piece of an epic about Nabopolassar (chapter 7) in which the heroic role of that king in founding the Chaldaean dynasty is described. The second fragment (chapter 8) mentions Evil-Merodach and the narrative may have included the reign of Nabonidus and perhaps even that of Cyrus. The contents of the third fragment (chapter 9) defy any precise dating. A text which must also be mentioned here, since it has the general form and style of a Babylonian historical epic, is the verse account of Nabonidus. However it is a unique composition in that it is essentially a religio-political tract only thinly disguised as an epic. It was written in the interests of the Marduk priests at Babylon with the intention of discrediting and castigating Nabonidus and gaining favour with the conqueror of Babylonia, Cyrus.[14]

The Babylonian historical epics are tendentious works. In each prevails the theme of the supremacy of Marduk over the gods and the ill-fate that befalls a Babylonian king who neglects or ignores his deity's cult. This view is particularly apparent in the Adad-shuma-usur epic, which necessitates some discussion. The king seems to be guilty of some offence against Marduk and is compelled to confess his sins and perform pious deeds. Clearly Marduk is here supreme god (*bēl bēlē* 'lord of lords'), followed in importance by the god of Borsippa[15] and the god of Cuthah. Now, as Lambert has convincingly argued, Marduk was not officially recognized as 'king of the

12 The text, K 3426, was published by King, CT 13, 48 and cf. Winckler, Altorientalische Forschungen 1 (Leipzig 1893–7) pp 542–3 (the tablet number is incorrect in this reference).

13 A possible epic fragment that might be assigned to this period was published by Gurney, STT 2, no. 366 and cf. Deller, Or.n.s. 34 (1965) p. 461 and Reiner, JNES 26 (1967) p. 197.

14 The text was published by Smith, BHT pp. 27–97 and pls. 5–10. For bibliography see Grayson, ABC p. 57, n. 62 and addenda and Borger, HKL p. 490. Even more curious is the late text called 'Nebuchadnezzar King of Justice' (cf. chapter 1, n. 6).

15 Lambert has stated that the god of Borsippa in the second millennium was not Nabu, nor is his recognition as the son of Marduk attested before the first millennium. (See Mitteilungen des Instituts für Orientforschung 12 [1966] pp. 43–8 and cf. BiOr 23 [1966] p. 164b. Also see Borger, BiOr 28 [1971] p. 22, n. 5.) The god of Borsippa is not mentioned by name in this epic (see iii 26–30 and the commentary to iii 27).

gods' until the reign of Nebuchadnezzar I, a century later;[16] thus the theological assumptions in the Adad-shuma-usur epic are anachronistic.[17] This is also true of the Kurigalzu epic (see chapter 5), where Marduk has a prominent position.[18] The significance of this for the date of composition will be taken up in a moment. The supremacy of Marduk is also the theme of the epics about the Chaldaean dynasty. In the Nabopolassar epic all credit for the foundation of the dynasty was attributed to him. The improper behaviour of Evil-Merodach towards Marduk and his cult described in the second epic fragment of this period speaks for itself.

The copies of the Babylonian historical epics preserved all come from the late period. With the exception of the Nebuchadnezzar I epic, the quotations from the Kurigalzu epic in Chronicle P, and the Nabonidus verse account, all were copied by similar hands. In other words, all of the epic material published in this book appears to represent a small part of a section of a Late Babylonian library in which were kept historical epics about Babylonian kings that had been copied and collected by a group of learned Babylonians.

There can be no certainty about the date of the original composition of the Babylonian historical epics but tentative termini can be established, and within these termini probable periods will be pro-

16 Lambert, 'The Reign of Nebuchadnezzar I: A Turning Point in the History of Ancient Mesopotamian Religion' in W.S. McCullough (ed.), The Seed of Wisdom: Essays in Honour of T.J. Meek (Toronto 1964) pp. 3–13.

17 There is evidence that in the late Kassite period Marduk's kingship was gaining popular support; the personal name *Marduk-šar-ilāni* 'Marduk is king of the gods' is attested in the reign of Kudur-Enlil (before Adad-shuma-usur) (see ibid. p. 8). But the assumption of the epic is that Marduk's coronation had received official sanction. This is hard to accept for a time when even the statue of the god was absent; it had been transported to Assyria by Tukulti-Ninurta I and was not returned until long after the death of Adad-shuma-usur (see Grayson, ABC Chronicle 22 [Chronicle P] iv 12f). Unless a new statue had been fabricated, the long description in the epic of prayers to and commands from Marduk in Esagil are ludicrous in a period when the divine statue was absent. A late copy of a royal inscription of Adad-shuma-usur is also relevant for in this text Marduk is not at the top of the pantheon; the order of the gods is Anu, Enlil, and Marduk. The text, BM 36042 (SP III, 587) (line 3, collated, clearly reads: ^{d}IŠKUR-MU-ŠE[Š]), is said to be from a bronze statue. It was originally published by Winckler, Sumer und Akkad, Mitteilungen des Akademisch-orientalischen Vereins zu Berlin 1887, p. 19, n. 6; cf. Winckler, Untersuchungen zur altorientalischen Geschichte (Leipzig 1889) p. 46 and Brinkman, ZA 59 (1969) p. 234.

18 Cf. Grayson, ABC Chronicle 22 (Chronicle P) iii 8f. The same theme, the supremacy of Marduk, is used anachronistically in the Weidner chronicle (see Grayson, ABC Chronicle 19).

posed. For the epics about second-millennium kings a basic terminus a quo is provided by the theme of the supremacy of Marduk, which means composition can be no earlier than the late twelfth century, and the date of Nebuchadnezzar I's accession, 1126 B.C., will be used for convenience. For these same epics the following termini ad quem are proposed: Kurigalzu epic – 783 B.C. (?);[19] Adad-shuma-usur epic – 1000 B.C.(?);[20] Nebuchadnezzar I epic – 612 B.C.[21] Within this time range there are two periods for which there is evidence of literary activity.[22] The first is the reign of Nebuchadnezzar I[23] and the second is the early part of the first millennium.[24] Although the composition of each of these texts may have occurred at any time within their respective termini it is somewhat more probable that it took place in one of these two periods. Moreover the reign of Nebuchadnezzar I is the more likely possibility because the theme of the supremacy of Marduk is known in other literary works about that time. For the epics about the Chaldaean dynasty the terminus a quo in each case is the accession date of the king involved. Since all texts are known from 'late' copies no precise terminus ad quem can be established. One exception is the Nabonidus verse account, for which the most obvious date is about the time of the capture of Babylon by Cyrus in 539 B.C. It is quite possible that the other epics were also composed at this time. But it must be emphasized that the

19 This terminus is very uncertain. It is based on the assumption that Chronicle P, our main source for the Kurigalzu epic to which the fragment published in chapter 5 may also belong, existed at the time of the composition of the synchronistic history. The synchronistic history was probably written shortly after the death of Adad-nerari III (810–783 B.C.). See Grayson, ABC chapter 6.

20 This terminus is also very uncertain. It is based on the use of a Middle Babylonian word for 'noble' (see the commentary to ii 15 and for approximate dates of the Middle Babylonian dialect see von Soden, GAG §2e). But the author of the epic could have lived after the Middle Babylonian period and merely employed an archaic word for authenticity.

21 The sole exemplar of the epic comes from Kouyunjik.

22 There may, of course, have been others for which no evidence has yet come to light.

23 See Lambert, 'The Reign of Nebuchadnezzar I'; Brinkman, PKB pp. 114–15; and Grayson, ABC appendix B sub Nebuchadnezzar I.

24 The Era epic was composed during this time. For a bibliography and discussion of the various dates proposed see Cagni, L'Epopea di Erra pp. 37–45. Most recently von Soden, UF 3 (1971) pp. 255–6 has stated that it dates to 765–763 B.C. For a more modest example of literary effort in the eighth century see Lambert, Journal of the American Oriental Society 88 (1968) pp. 123–30.

suggested dates for the composition of the Babylonian historical epics are all tentative.

That scribes of the Persian or Seleucid eras continued to copy epics about earlier Babylonian kings is no accident. One of the chief functions of the scribe at all times was to preserve the cultural heritage; this was especially true in periods when foreign influences threatened the very existence of Babylonian civilization.

5

Historical Epic Fragment about the Kassite Period

The fragment (BM 35322 = SP II, 893) is a small piece of a late Babylonian copy of an historical epic about the Kassite period. A clue to a more precise date is provided by the reference to Enlil-kidinni. There are two known officials in Kassite times who bore this name. One lived during the reigns of Karahardash, Nazibugash, Burnaburiash II, and Kurigalzu II.[1] The other lived about a century and a half later at the time of Adad-shuma-usur.[2] Until more text is available for the epic it is impossible to say which Enlil-kidinni and which period of time is the concern of the composition.[3] But it seems to me somewhat more probable that the first Enlil-kidinni – reigns of Burnaburiash II to Kurigalzu II – is involved. Extracts from an epic about Kurigalzu appear in Chronicle P[4] and among the events described is a conflict with Elam. The epic fragment under discussion also concerns an Elamo-Babylonian encounter and one wonders if this is not only about the same period and events but possibly a piece of the same epic. The second Enlil-kidinni lived in the time of

1 See K. Balkan, Ankara Üniversitesi Dil ve Tarih-Coğrafya Fakültesi Dergisi 2 (1943) pp. 45–55; Türk Tarih Kurumu, Belleten 12 (1948) p. 747, n. 72; B. Landsberger, Brief des Bischofs von Esagila, Mededelingen der Koninklijke Nederlandse Akademie van Wetenschappen, Afd. Letterkunde, Nieuwe Reeks, Deel 28, no. 6 (Amsterdam 1965) p. 77; and Sollberger, Journal of the American Oriental Society 88 (1968) pp. 191–2.

2 His estate was the subject of a legal dispute, the history of which is described in a *kudurru* (L.W. King Babylonian Boundary-Stones [London 1912] no. 3) from the time of Meli-shihu.

3 It is possible there were other people of this name for whom no evidence has yet come to light.

4 See Grayson, ABC chapter 6 and Chronicle 22 (Chronicle P) ii and iii.

Adad-shuma-usur, for whose reign no Elamite conflict is attested. But in view of our scanty knowledge of the period too much weight should not be attached to this.[5] Thus, although there is no cogent reason to reject the time of Adad-shuma-usur for the epic fragment, the evidence is slightly in favour of the reign of Kurigalzu II, and it is even possible that the fragment comes from the same epic for which extracts are preserved in Chronicle P.

A description of the content is difficult because the fragment seems to contain only parts of two columns of a four-column tablet. In ii(?) 1–11 there are traces of direct speech which conclude with reference to an 'enemy' and a throne. The remainder, ii(?) 12–19, is a third-person narration about an attack, the ominous darkening of the sky, and an Elamite who retreats but is captured by the king's sons.

iii(?) 1–5 contains a command to bring something, apparently from the Elamite woman who is mentioned later, to the daughter of Enlil-kidinni. iii(?) 6 is the beginning of a reply to the command. The Elamite woman[6] appears to have been guilty of some impious act. The speaker promises to carry out the commission to bring away her 'pectorals' and give them to the daughter of Enlil-kidinni (7f.). In iii(?) 9–15 the speaker describes how he then slew the Elamitess and flung her corpse down from the wall.[7]

The fragment, which measures c. 9 x 15 cm., is from the right side of a large tablet. The identification of obverse and reverse is uncertain. The original tablet probably had two columns on each side since iii(?) 5–8 and 12, with slight restorations at the beginning, seem to be complete lines. The scribal relationship of the copy to other late copies of epic texts has been discussed in chapter 4. Palaeographically it is similar to the copy of the Adad-shuma-usur epic; the width of the columns was probably the same on both tablets; but since this fragment is slightly thicker its original was probably a bit larger.

5 Just before Adad-shuma-usur's time there had been Elamite raids on Babylonia (see Chronicle P iv 14–24) and within half a century of his death Elam had brought the Kassite dynasty to an end. Thus it would not be at all surprising if evidence should eventually appear of Elamo-Babylonian hostilities during the reign of Adad-shuma-usur.

6 The identity of this woman is unknown but she seems to have been a princess or queen. Note the reference to a Suhaean woman in the Adad-shuma-usur epic (chapter 6) iv 10. The fact that a woman bears the name 'Elamitess' (*E-la-mi-tum*) in a Middle Babylonian document from Dur-Kurigalzu (see Gurney, Iraq 11 [1949] p. 147, no. 8, r. 24 and cf. p. 138) indicates that women of this period could simply be referred to by a gentilic rather than a personal name.

7 Cf. the fate of Jezebel as described in 2 Kings 9:30–7.

Thus less than a quarter of the original text is preserved. There are some noteworthy scribal features.[8]

8 a/ *ma-ḫaṣ* for *maḫāṣi* in iii(?) 9.
b/ *iq-ṭa-bi* in ii(?) 12 and also in BM 45684 (chapter 9) r.(?) 11 and BM 34062 (SP 158 + SP II, 962 'Kedorlaomer Text') r. 20 (collated) is a late feature. Cf. von Soden, GAG §29e.
c/ Use of masculine suffixes for feminine: In iii(?) 7 -*ka* has been used for -*ki* and in iii(?) 12–14 -*šu* has been used for -*ša*. Thus I have assumed that -*šu* stands for -*ša* in 10f. (cf. 19–20) and -*su* for -*si* in 10–11. That is, they all refer to the Elamite woman.
d/ Aleph written at the end of the plural verb form in ii(?) 6.

ii(?)

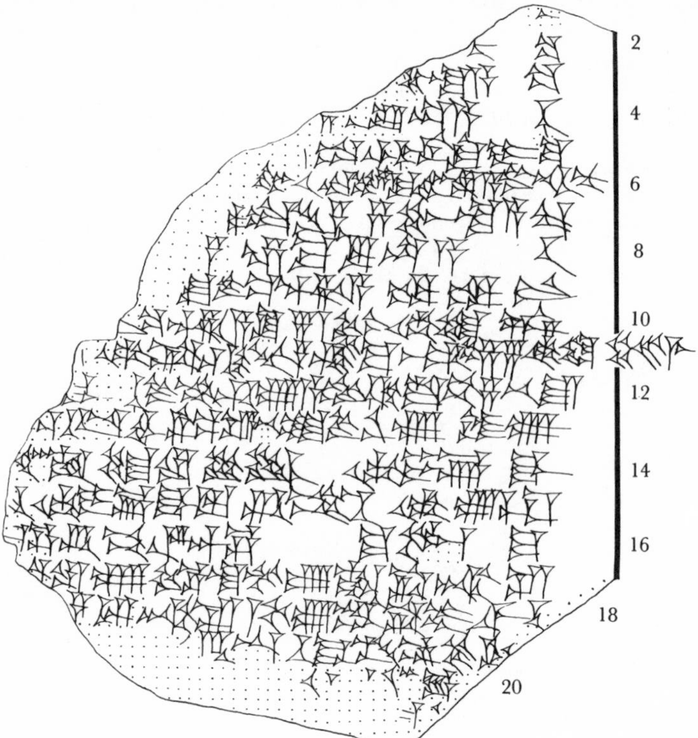

Obverse (?) of BM 35322 (SP II, 893)

iii(?)

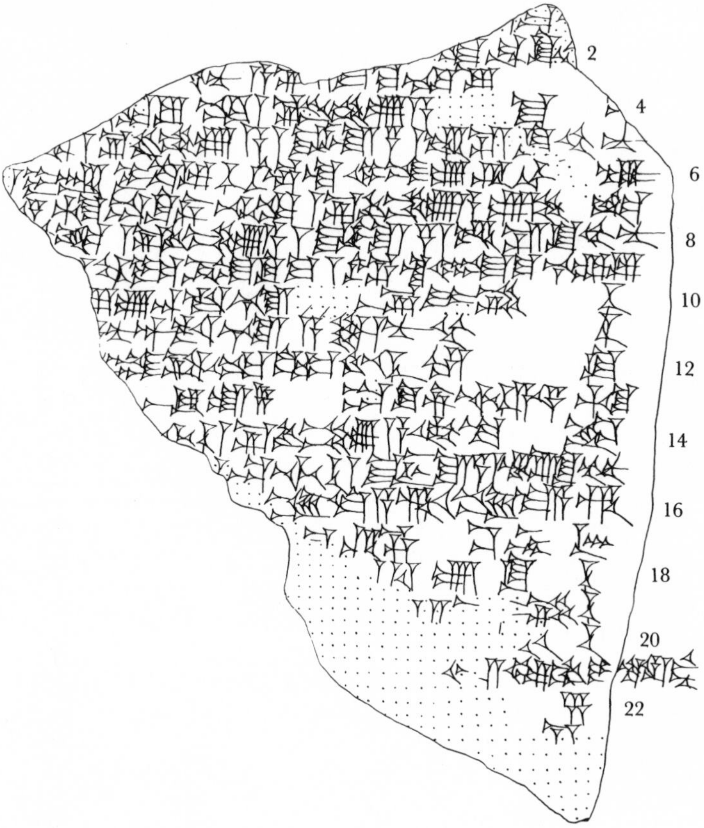

Reverse (?) of BM 35322 (SP II, 893)

TRANSLITERATION

Obverse (?) ii (?)

Lacuna

1 [… …]-⌜*tú*(?)⌝

2 [… …] x-*tú*

3 [… … *za*(?)]-*bu-la-a-tú*

4 [… … GAR^{a}]^{a} ⌜*ba*⌝-*lu na-a-šú*

5 [… …] x du igi pa *ni-di-i-ma*(?)

6 [… …]-' *u na-as-ku-'* ŠUB^{a} *pagrē*(adda)-*šú-nu*

7 [… …] *imērī*^{meš} *šá za-bu-la-a-tú*

8 [… …] GAR^{a} *ba-lu na-a-šú*

9 [… …] ki ^{lú}GIŠ.AN.ḪA.A *izzanakkar*(?gù.gù)^{ár}

10 [… …] ^{lú}GIŠ.AN.ḪA.A KI(?)-*iá ana* ^{lú}*nakri ul-tu* MAR(?)^{u}

11 [… …] x *ul ta-nam-din ša-nam-ma ina* ^{giš}*kussê-iá ul tu-še-eš-šib*

12 [… … *ma-ḫ*]*ar*(?)-*šú* ^{lú}DU$_8$.ḪU.Ú.A *šarru iq-ṭa-bi ṣa-bat-su*

13 [… …]an(?) kap pi ni *is-dir šil-taḫ ana* ^{lú}*nakri ú-ṣu-ú*

14 [… …]-' *it-tu-ru aḫu aḫa-šú ul i-dag-gal*

15 [… …]-x-*šú ul i-dag-gal ib-ri tap-pu-šú ul ú-mas-si*

16 [… …]x *e-re-bi pān*(igi^{u}) *šamê*^{e} *ma-li*(?)-*ma*

17 [… …] x-*ru-ú* ^{lú}*E-la-mu-ú it-ta-bal-kit*

18 [… …]-*šá ib-bal-kit ana šadû*^{ú} *it-ta-kan panē-šú*

19 [… … *i*]*k*(?)-*tal-du-šú mārē*^{meš} *šarri še-gu-*[*ú*(?)]

20 [… …] x x x ITI [x x]

21 [… …] x […]

Lacuna

ii(?) 3f. Cf. ii(?) 7f. *za-bu-la-a-tú* is an otherwise unattested word derived from *zabālu* 'to bear.'

ii(?) 6 ŠUB^{a} *pagrē*(adda)-*šú-nu*: Cf. iii(?) 12.

ii(?) 9f. ^{lú}GIŠ.AN.ḪA.A is otherwise unknown. Cf. the note to ii(?) 12.

TRANSLATION

Obverse (?) ii (?)

Lacuna

1–2 Too broken for translation

3 [… …] pack-[*asses*]

4 [… … he establis]hed without our permission.

5 [… …] … we knew/know

6 [… …] and were thrown down, their corpses were flung down.

7 [… …] pack-asses

8 [… …] he established without our permission.

9 [… …] *with* … he *continually talks*

10 [… …] … *with* me to the enemy …

11 [… …] you must not give/allow, another on my throne you must not set.'

12 [… … *bef*]*ore* him … the king commanded that he be seized.

13 [… …] … he/we arrayed, arrows shot out at the enemy.

14 [… …] returned, one will/does not see another,

15 [… …] his […] will/does not see, friend will/does not discern companion,

16 [With a swarm of] locusts the face of heaven was/is *filled* and

17 [… …] … the Elamite retreated

18 [… …] he retreated, he headed towards the mountains.

19 [… …] they *overtook/captured* him, the sons of the king were *angry*.

20–21 Too broken for translation

Lacuna

ii(?) 12 ^{lú}DU$_8$.ḪU.Ú.A: Cf. *bīt* ^{lú}DU$_8$Ú.A in iii(?) 4, 5, 7, 8, 14. Whether the two are connected is unknown, as are their reading and meaning. Cf. the note to ii(?) 9f.

ii(?) 15 For *mussû* 'to discern' see Falkenstein, Literarische Keilschrifttexte aus Uruk (Berlin 1931) p. 13 and Lambert, BWL p. 322, note to 127.

Reverse (?) iii (?)

Lacuna

1 [......] x x x [x]

2 [...... t]um diš ba(?) *ki-din-*[*nu*]

3 [...... *ki*]-*din-nu* a É/DAN/TA/UŠ x x ma ka lu [x]

4 [......] x ka(?) ib ka *ana bīt* ^{lú}DU$_8$.Ú.A *šu-b*[*il*(?)]

5 [*šu*(?)-*b*]*il*(?) *ana bīt* ^{lú}DU$_8$.Ú.A. *ana mārat-su šá* ^{md}*En-líl-ki-din-nu*

6 x-*i* MAḪ *i-te-ep-šú* ^{SAL}*E-la-mi-tum ú-dal/tal-lim* ^{d}*Nabû*

7 [*a-p*]*aṭ-ṭar du-di-ni-ti-ka ana bīt* ^{lú}DU$_8$.Ú.A. *ú-še-bil*

8 [*ú-š*]*e-bil ana bīt* ^{lú}DU$_8$.Ú.A *ana mārat-su šá* ^{md}*En-líl-ki-din-nu*

9 [...] x *pi-i* ^{giš}*qašti ad-di-ma ana* ^{SAL}*E-la-mi-tum ana ma-ḫaṣ al-lik*

10 [... *l*]*u-ú an-da-ḫas-su ina* KAL i GAB ŠÚ

11 [... *da*]*n*(?)-*nu an-da-ḫas-su a-šar là balāṭi*$_3$-*šú*

12 [^{SAL}*E-la-m*]*i-tum ultu muḫḫi dūri pagar*(adda)-*šú* ŠUB^{di}

13 [......] *ina kin*(?)-*ṣi-iá du-di-ni-ti-šú a-paṭ-ṭar*

14 [... *du-di-ni-t*]*i-šú ana bīt* ^{lú}DU$_8$.Ú.A *ul-te-bil*

15 [......] x-*na-ti-šú ana mārat-su šá* ^{md}*En-líl-ki-din-nu*

16 [......] *zik-kar-ri u zik-kar-ri*

17 [...... *az-m*]*a-re-e* ^{giš}BAN^{meš}

18 [......] x ú ki šú

19 [......] x ⌜KAL(?) i⌝ GAB ŠÚ

20 [......] ⌜*là*⌝ [*b*]*alāṭi*$_3$-*šú*

21 [......] x *ana*(?) *muḫḫi* LUGAL *i-te-ru-ub*

22 [......]-*iá*

23 [......] x

Lacuna

iii(?) 4f. Cf. 7f. and 13–15.

iii(?) 4 ^{lú}DU$_8$.Ú.A: See the commentary to ii(?) 12.

Reverse (?) iii (?)

Lacuna

1 [... ...] ...

2 [... ...] ... divine prote[ction]

3 [... ... Enlil-ki]dinnu/divine] protection ... ...

4 [... ...] bring your ... to the house of ...

5 [*Brin*]*g* to the house of ... to the daughter of Enlil-kidinnu.'

6 '... they made. The Elamite woman ... Nabu.

7 "[I] will undo your pectorals, I will bring to the house of ...

8 [I] will bring to the house of ... to the daughter of Enlil-kidinnu."

9 [*According to*] the command I threw down the bow and I went against the Elamite woman to smite (her).

10 [...] I smote her, ...

11 [...*str*]*ong*, I smote her in a fatal spot.

12 [The Elam]ite woman, her corpse I threw down from the wall.

13 [I] *kneeled down* to undo her pectorals.

14 [...] her [pectoral]s to the house of ... I took.

15 [*I took*] her ...s to the daughter of Enlil-kidinnu.'

16 [... ...] *men here, men there*

17 [... ... la]nces, bows

18 [... ...] ...

19 [... *I/he smote her*], ...

20 [... *I/he smote her in a*] fatal [*spot*].

21 [... ...] thereagainst the king entered.

22 [... ...] my [...]

23 [... ...] ...

Lacuna

iii(?) 6 *ú-dal/tal-lim*: No suitable root is known.

iii(?) 10f. Cf. iii(?) 19f.

6

Adad-shuma-usur Epic

With the publication of the Adad-shuma-usur epic the reign (c. 1222/09–1193/80 B.C.) of this late Kassite king comes more sharply into focus. It was a period in which Adad-shuma-usur, having been placed on the throne by a revolution, could exercise unaccustomed influence over Assyria. But, apart from this, little was known of the long reign until the discovery of the epic. Unfortunately the text is badly broken and not even all the preserved text is intelligible. But at least the fragmentary remains enable us not only to add an important piece of information to our reconstruction of the history of the period but to appreciate the prominent position of this king in Babylonian tradition.

In brief, the epic seems to describe a successful rebellion by officers and nobles of Babylon against Adad-shuma-usur. It would appear that the cause of the rebellion was neglect of Marduk and Babylon, since after the rebellion the penitent king confesses his sins to Marduk and thereafter carries out the restoration of the temple Esagil. Such a rebellion is otherwise unattested for Adad-shuma-usur's reign. It is known that he himself came to the throne as the result of a revolution[1] and further that he supported Ninurta-apil-Ekur in his bid to take over Assyria.[2] Indeed, his was a long and tumultuous reign to which must now be added yet another major crisis. There is no clue as to the date in Adad-shuma-usur's reign when the rebellion took place.[3]

1 See Grayson, ABC Chronicle 22 (Chronicle P) iv 8–9. The rebels were 'the Akkadian officers of Karduniash.' In this epic they are called 'officers' (*rabûti*) or 'lords' (*bēlū*) and 'nobles of Babylon' (*banû Bābili*). (See ii 15 and 19. Also cf. iii 7.) Thus the two rebellions may have been instigated by the same group, viz. the old, non-Kassite, nobility of Babylon.

2 See Grayson, ABC Chronicle 21 (Synchronistic History) ii 3–8. Cf. Brinkman, PKB p. 87, n. 453.

3 It is not absolutely certain that a rebellion is described in this epic. See the commentary to i 7. However, even if the word discussed there cannot be interpreted as I have suggested, the sequence of events in columns i and ii seems to indicate a rebellion.

With regard to the content, it should be noted that the entire first column is poorly preserved and this outline is to be judged accordingly. i 1–11 is a description, either in the first or third person, of someone going down to the palace garden, apparently for the purpose of organizing a revolution. There the rebel leader gathers fugitives to his cause and offers praise to Bel (Marduk); the passage concludes with an enigmatic statement about the king. i 12 is apparently an introduction to the direct speech of i 13–19. Someone now seems to be addressing the rebel leader. Reference is then made to a descent into the palace garden, to lords and killing, and to seeking rebellion. Further references to dirty garments, to wiping feet, and to illuminating the land are equally puzzling.

Direct speech is again introduced (i 20) and the passage (i 21–9) seems to be the speech of an official whose name is unfortunately mutilated. He says he went down to the gardener to seek something and then, strangely enough, refers to a launderer and washing (reminiscent of the 'dirty garments' mentioned earlier in the column). The remainder of the speech, however, describes military activities and the name of king Adad-shuma-usur appears. There was apparently a rebellion both within and without the palace. One wonders if the official who made this speech was the rebel leader.

In the remains of column i a new speech (i 31f.) seems to be introduced (by i 30). There follows a lacuna of indeterminate size. The beginning of column ii is also badly mutilated but the references to a launderer (ii 7) and rebelling (ii 10) are noteworthy.

The understandable portion of column ii seems to be a narration of the events after the apparent rebellion against Adad-shuma-usur. The revolution, in which the officers and nobles of Babylon took a prominent role, seems to have been successful, but the king was still alive. ii 11–13 may be a speech of the officers and nobles to the king. ii 14 seems to introduce direct speech (ii 15–18) of the king. The king asks that he be admitted to the 'palace' to pray to Marduk:

> That me alone [he] might bring me out, me alone
> he might bring [me] in [...]
> That me alone [he] might cause to stand in the
> assembly of the people.

It is not at all clear what this means. Someone, perhaps the officers and nobles, now speaks (ii 19–21), granting the king permission to enter and pray. There follows (ii 22–31) a description of the king's entry to Esagil, the confession of his sins to Bel (Marduk), a reference to people under divine protection (*kidinnu*), and the offering of sacrifices.

In brief, column ii suggests that although the rebellion against Adad-shuma-usur was successful, the rebels spared the king because he was penitent for his wrong, viz. some kind of insult to or neglect of Marduk. Having been spared, the king requests and is granted permission to try and make amends to the god.

After a break at the beginning of column iii there is a detailed description of the restoration and refurbishment of Esagil. It appears that two men, Remut and Shar-ilua, donated silver and gave directions for its use in the renovation of the temple (iii 8–17). This passage is followed by a repetition of the instructions, this time in first person (iii 18–23). Presumably the king is speaking but the addressee is unfortunately not identified.

With the restoration of Esagil the narrative returns to the third person to describe the king's departure from Babylon (iii 24–5) and his journey to Borsippa, where he enters the temple, confesses his sins, and does some construction (iii 26–30). From Borsippa he goes to Cuthah, enters the temple Emeslam, and prays to Nergal (iii 31–4). Such a pilgrimage, Babylon to Borsippa to Cuthah, is well attested for some of the Kalach kings of Assyria, viz. Shalmaneser III, Shamshi-Adad V, and Adad-nerari III.[4] Among the Chaldaean kings of Babylonia the sequence of the patron deities – Marduk, Nabu, and Nergal – of these cities is attested[5] and Nebuchadnezzar II, in describing restoration of various temples, puts Esagil, Ezida, and Emeslam first and in that order.[6] This epic provides the earliest evidence for this ranking and for the pilgrimage from Babylon to Borsippa to Cuthah.

At the end of column iii and the beginning of column iv there is another lacuna. The text of column iv, which is as badly preserved as column i, is difficult to interpet. At the beginning (iv 1–12) various workmen (farmer, potter, launderer) and the 'Suhaean woman' appear.[7] Is it possible that this was a description of income assigned

4 In addition to these cities Tiglath-pileser III also went to make sacrifices at Sippar, Nippur, Kish, Dilbat, and Uruk. See Grayson, ABC appendix B, sub Shamshi-Adad V for details. Also cf. E. von Weiher, Nergal, AOAT 11 (1971) p. 99.

5 Langdon, VAB 4, pp. 66–9 (Nabopolassar); VAB 4, p. 234 ii 27f. and p. 260:49 (Nabonidus) (cf. Tadmor in H.G. Güterbock and T. Jacobsen (eds.), Studies in Honor of Benno Landsberger on his Seventy-Fifth Birthday, Assyriological Studies 16 [Chicago 1965] p. 359, n. 42, and E. von Weiher, Nergal p. 68, n. 1). Regarding Nabu's position as god of Borsippa see chapter 4, n. 15.

6 Langdon, VAB 4, pp. 90–2; also cf. pp. 108, 168–70, and 180–2.

7 Also note the Suhaean(s) in iv 18. These people are attested sporadically from Old Babylonian to Neo-Assyrian times. See Brinkman, PKB pp. 183–4, n. 1127.

to temple personnel by the king? The king is mentioned in iv 13. The next passage (iv 14–24) contains a description of districts and grants ('he gave'). The palace, Esagil, and Duranki (temple complex at Nippur) appear and one wonders if this was a description of major allotments of land to temples (and possibly also to the successful rebels). The phenomenon of royal land grants is well-known in Kassite and post-Kassite Babylonia although the grand scale involved in column iv, if this in fact is what is being narrated, is unusual.

The remaining few lines which are preserved (iv 25–32) begin with a blessing and this may be a conclusion or summation to the epic.

Approximately one-third to one-half of the inscription is missing. Originally the tablet was square, measuring c. 19 x 19 cms. What remains of the tablet has been reconstructed by means of several joins: BM 34644 (SP II, 127 + 81–7–6, 191) is an old museum join; to this Lambert joined BM 34104 (SP 204), 34126 (SP 228), and 34339 (SP 454); to these I joined BM 34219 (SP 325), 34230 (SP 336), and 34657 (SP II, 140); and Sollberger added 34256 (SP 363). Pinches copied BM 34657 and this copy was published by Walker as CT 51, no. 77. None of the other fragments has ever been published. There are several features typical for a text copied in the late period[8] and some scribal errors.[9] The scribal relationship of the copy to other late copies of epic texts has been discussed in chapter 4.

8 a/ *-ku* for *-ka* (*-ka* also appears) in i 18, 19, iii 27.
b/ *-mu* for *-ma* (*-ma* also appears) in iii 29(?), 31.
c/ *-nu* for *-ni* (first person suffix) (*-ni* also appears) in i 22 and ii 15.
d/ *Bar-sìp*: this orthography is attested only in late Assyrian and Babylonian texts (see W. von Soden and W. Röllig, Das Akkadische Syllabar, Analecta Orientalia 42 [2nd ed. Rome 1967], no. 228 and cf. Borger, JNES 19 [1960] p. 51).
e/ aleph written at the end of plural verb forms in i 14, ii 24, iii 10(!), 11, iv 22.

9 i 7(?), 21(?), iii 10, 12, 19, iv 21(?).

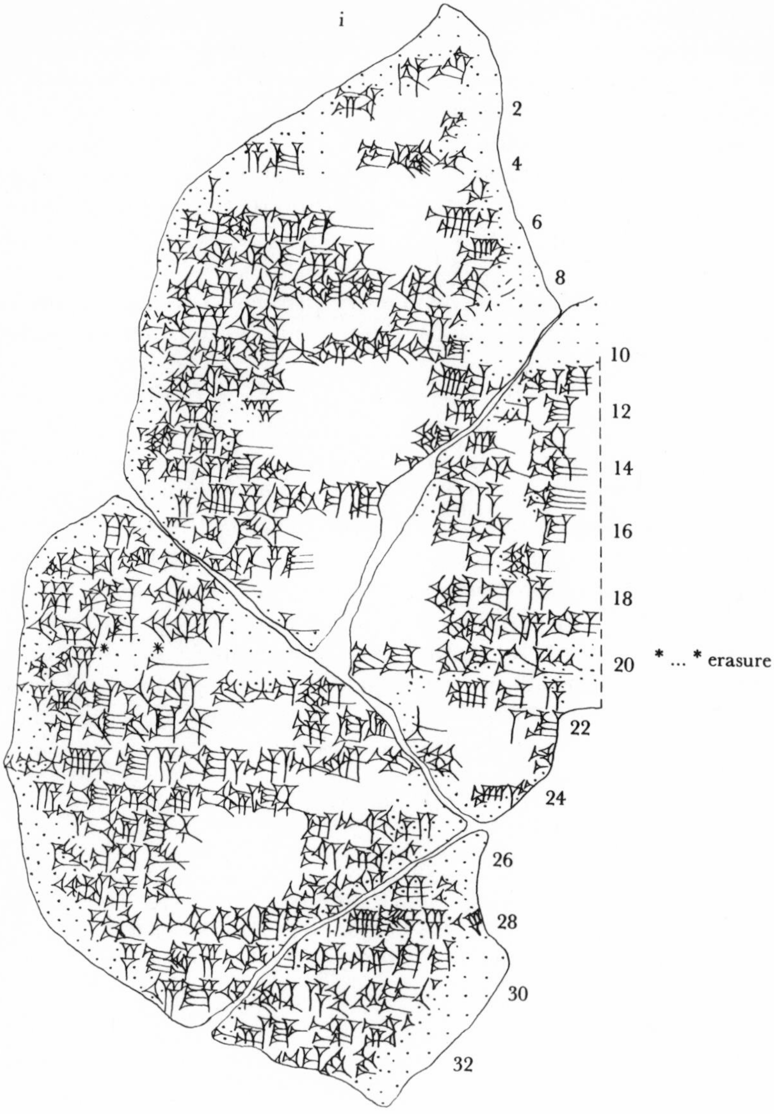

Obverse of BM 34104 (SP 204) + 34126 (SP 228) + 34219 (SP 325) + 34230 (SP 336) + 34256 (SP 363) + 34339 (SP 454) + 34644 (SP II, 127 + 81-7-6, 191) + 34657 (SP II, 140)

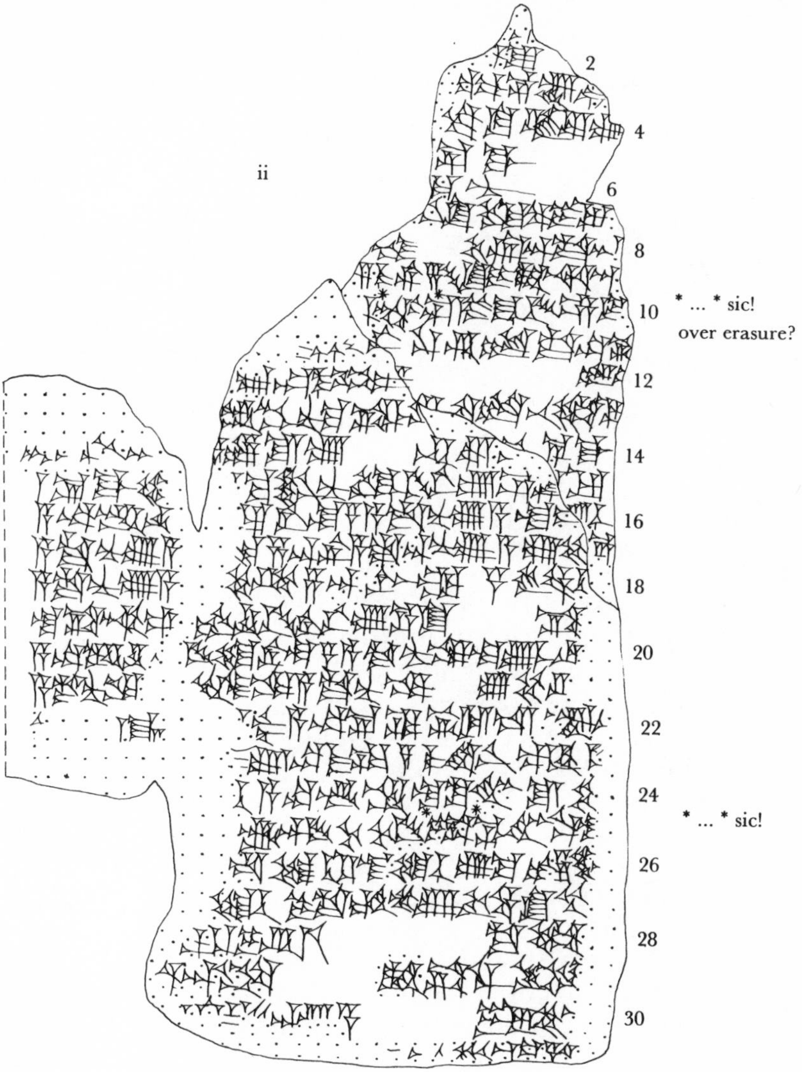

Obverse of BM 34104 (SP 204) + 34126 (SP 228) + 34219 (SP 325) + 34230 (SP 336) + 34256 (SP 363) + 34339 (SP 454) + 34644 (SP II, 127 + 81-7-6, 191) + 34657 (SP II, 140)

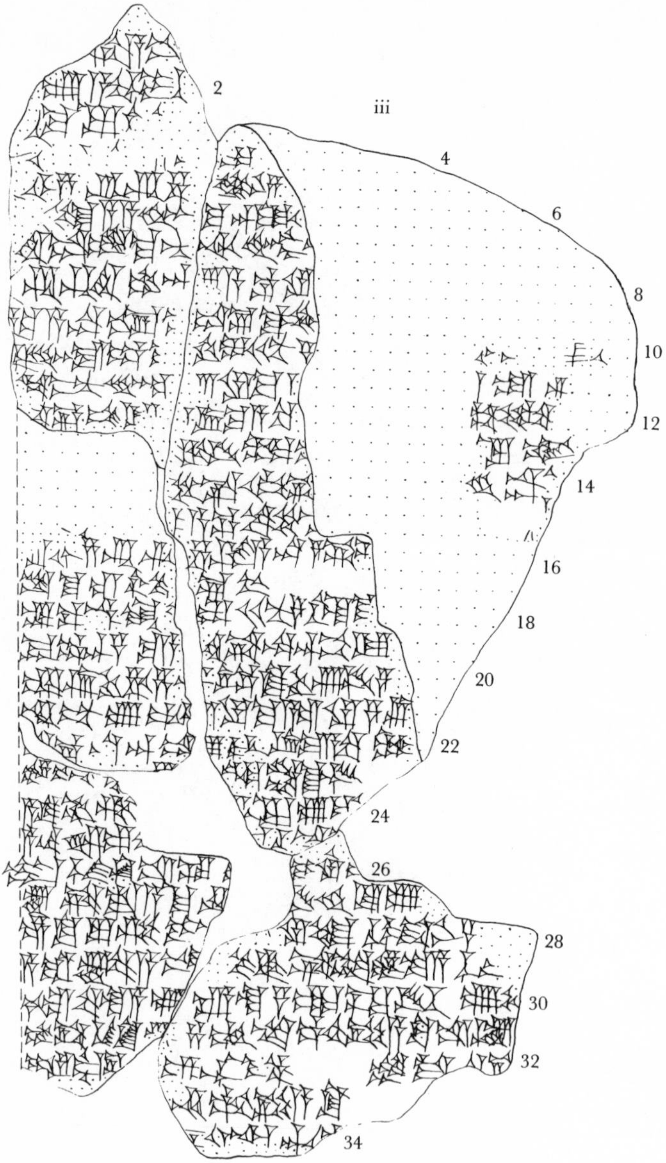

Reverse of BM 34104 (SP 204) + 34126 (SP 228) + 34219 (SP 325) + 34230 (SP 336) + 34256 (SP 363) + 34339 (SP 454) + 34644 (SP II, 127 + 81-7-6, 191) + 34657 (SP II, 140)

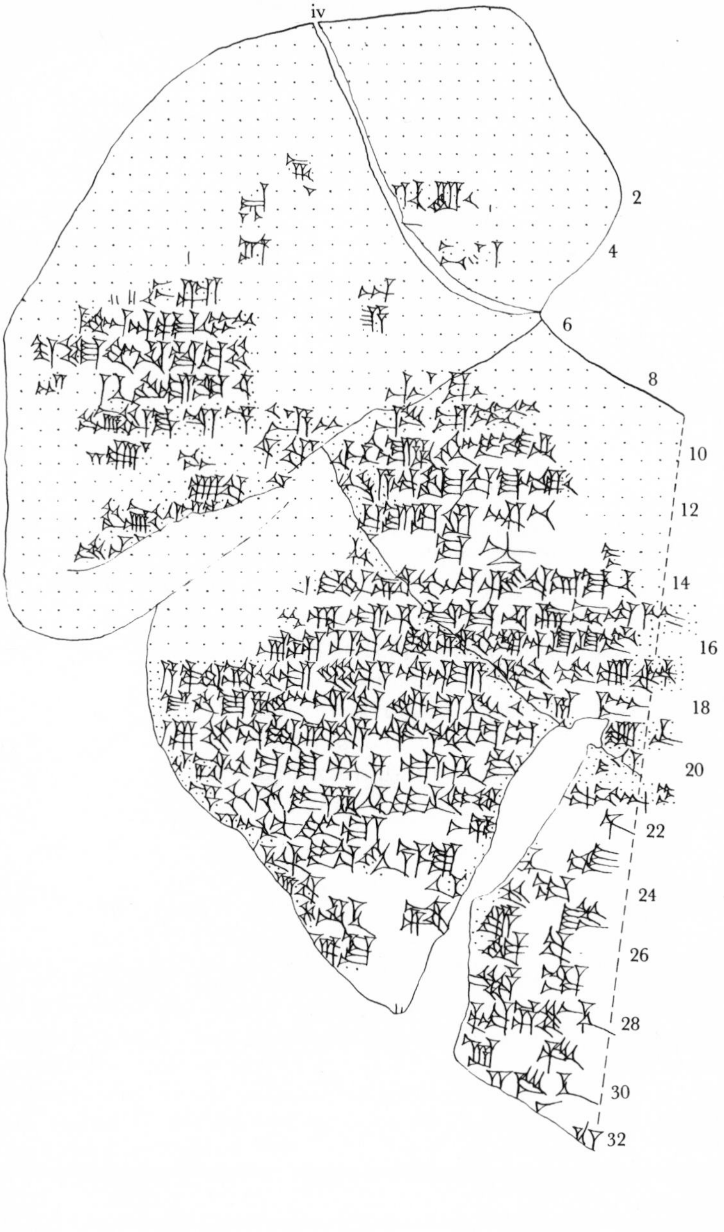

Reverse of BM 34104 (SP 204) + 34126 (SP 228) + 34219 (SP 325) + 34230 (SP 336) + 34256 (SP 363) + 34339 (SP 454) + 34644 (SP II, 127 + 81-7-6, 191) + 34657 (SP II, 140)

TRANSLITERATION

i

Lacuna

1 [… …] x pi lam(?) […]
2 [… …] ta […]
3 [… …] *i*-[…]
4 [… …] a ku *i-nam-din*-[x]
5 [… …] x r[u x]
6 [… …] x *kirî ekallim ú-r*[*i*(?)-*du*(?)]

7 [… …]-*a na-bal-kát-ta-šú ú-b*[*a*(?)-*a*]
8 [… …] *mu-un-na-bi-tu-tu ul-te*-x-([x])
9 [… …] x *egirrâ*(inim.gar) *damqa*(sig$_5$) *i-za-a*[*m-mur*(?)]
10 [… …] x-*bi* ^{d}*Bēl tu-kul-ta-ka man-nu ki*-[*i*(?) x]
11 [… … *ḫa*(?)-*a*]*l*(?)-*le-e šarri ú-ma-a*[*k*]-*ka-ku*
12 [… … *i*]*t*(?)-*ta*-x-x *ri-gim-šu*
13 [… … *ana*] *kirî ekallim tu-ri-du*
14 [… …] *šá ur-ru-šu-' l*[*u*]-*bu-ši-ka*
15 [… …]-*iá*(?) *ú-ḫa-am-ma-ṭu* ([x]) *ma-a-tum*
16 [… …] x a x x *bēlē*^{meš}-*šú i-du-ku*
17 [… … i]t(?) x *šēpē*^{II}-*ka ta-maš-šá-áš kirâ*
18 [… …] x KÙ ni-*ku na-bal*-[*k*]*át tu-ba-a*
19 [… … *tu-ku*]*l*(?)-*ta-ku* niš dad x x *li-qa-a-ka*
20 [… …]-MUN-*iá-aš* ([…]) ^{lú}*ráb* ^{lú}GAL.DÙ^{meš}

i 6 The first sign does not look like *na* for [*a-n*]*a*. It might be DIŠ (for *ana*) with two horizontal strokes running over from the previous sign.
ú-r[*i*(?)-*du*(?)]: Cf. i 13 where the verb is subjunctive.

i 7 Cf. i 18. *nabalkattu* could also be translated 'ladder,' which would be a suitable means of illicit access to a garden. Similarly in i 25 *ibbalkit* might be translated 'he climbed over (into his palace).' However, the context of the last reference sounds military, as does the context of ii 10 in which *ibbalkit* also appears. A final decision must await recovery of more of this epic. At the end of i 18 *tu-ba-a* is clear. At the end of i 21 and possibly at the end of i 7 the scribe has written *ú-ma-a* but I have assumed he intended *ú-ba*!-*a*.

i 10 *man-nu ki*-[*i*(?) x]: Cf. the Nabopolassar epic (chapter 7) ii(?) 8.

i 11 Cf. i 27 and 28. The context and the verb *mukkuku* (otherwise it is attested in the D only in lexical texts) suggest a body-part as object. *ḫallū* seems the most probable restoration.

TRANSLATION

i

Lacuna

1–3 Too broken for translation

4 [... ...] ... he gives/will give [...]
5 [... ...] ... [...]
6 [*When/after* ... ...] ... *to* the garden of the palace I/he *went* [*down*],
7 [... ...] my [...] I/he sought his *rebellion/rebellion* against him.
8 [... ...] fugitives I/he caused to ...
9 [... ...] good reputation/utterances he *sin*[*gs*]/*will sin*[*g*]:
10 '[... ...] ... Bel, your help, who (*is*) *like* [*you*]?'
11 [... ... the *le*]*gs* of the king I/he/they *spread*(*s*)/will *spread*.
12 [... ... *he*] ... his shout.
13 '[*When/after* ... ... *to*] the garden of the palace you went down.
14 [... ...] that/which dirty are your garments.
15 [... ...] my [...] they (will) illuminate the land.
16 [... ...] ... his lords they killed.
17 [... ...] ... your feet, you (will) wipe off, the garden.
18 [... ...] your ... you sought *rebellion*.
19 [... ...] your [*he*]*lp* ... take for yourself!'
20 [... ...]-munyash, (...) chief of the ... s

i 13–19 With the change to second person one might assume direct speech.

i 15 Cf. Gilgamesh XI 104.

i 18 See the note to i 7.

i 20 A Kassite name with the element -MUN- in this position is otherwise unattested. But cf. *Nu-ni-ia-ši* Balkan, Kassitenstudien, American Oriental Series 37 (New Haven 1954), p. 75 and *Sa-nu-na-aš* ibid. p. 14, no. 2:7 and cf. p. 126.

^{lú}*ráb* ^{lú}GAL.DÙ^{meš}: For ^{lú}GAL.DÙ see San Nicolò, Beiträge zu einer Prosopographie neubabylonischer Beamten, Sitzungsberichte der Bayrischen Akademie der Wissenschaften, philosoph.-hist. Abteilung 1941/II/2 (Munich 1941), p. 68, n. 3, and von Soden, AHw p. 933a and cf. the commentary to ii 15.

21 [……] x šá gab *at-tar-du ana* ^{lú}*nukaribbi ú-ba*(?)*-a*
22 [……] x *ma*(?)*-tum* ^{lú}*ašlāku*(azalag) *un-de-sa-nu ana-ku*
23 [……] *mi-nu-ú šú-la-a-tum a-na* ^{md}*Adad-šuma-uṣur šar*[*ri*]

24 […*šú-l*]*a-a-tum šá ultu lìb-bi ekalli-šú* ([*la*(?)]) *ú-ṣ*[*u-ú*(?)]
25 [… *i-n*]*a*(?) [*l*]*ìb-bi ekalli-šú ib-bal-kit* […]
26 [……]$^{\text{meš giš}}$*narkabāti*^{meš} *iš-ta-k*[*a-an* …]
27 […… *ḫa*(?)*-al*(?)]*-le-e šarri ina kišādi-ka ú*-x […]
28 […… *ḫa*(?)*-al*(?)*-le*]-⌜*e*⌝ *šarri ina ti-ik-ki*(! tablet: DI)-*i*(?) ŠUB^{ú}
qabli-iá u(?) x […]
29 [……] *šá qabli-iá il-la-ka-an-ni di-ma*(?)-[*ti*(?) …]
30 [……] x *a-bur-ru-uš*$_{10}$ *a-mat pi-i* x […]
31 [……] *ina ekalli-ka ta*-x […]
32 [……] x *muḫ-ḫi* LÚ […]
Lacuna

ii

Lacuna
1 [……] x [……]
2 [……] x su [……]
3 [……] x pe e iḫ x [……]
4 [……] te di gi *lu-ú* [……]
5 [……] *ekallu* [……]
6 [……]-⌜*ku*⌝-*nu* [……]
7 [……] kak/ni *itti*(ki) ^{lú}*ašlāki*(azalag) *i-dab*-[*bu-ub*/*bu* ……]
8 [……]-*tum* ^{kur}*Kár-an-da-an*-[……]
9a [……] x *pa-ni-iá*
9b *ki-i it-ti* ^{md}[……]

i 21–9 This seems to be a speech by the official named in i 20. It is not clear where the speech ends but see the commentary to i 30–2.

i 21 See the commentary to i 7.

i 22 *un-de-sa-nu* = *undessânnu* and the root is *mesû*.

i 25 See the note to i 7.

i 27 See the commentary to i 11.

21 ‘[*When/after* ... ...] ... I went down to the gardener, I sought.
22 [... ...] ... the launderer (shall) cause(s) me to wash.
23 [... ...] what garrisons are on the side of Adad-shuma-usur, the king?
24 [... the gar]risons which did [*not*] *co*[*me out*] from his palace
25 [...] *rebelled* within his palace [...]
26 [... ...] chariots he established [...]
27 [... ... the *l*]*egs* of the king on your neck I/he [...]
28 [... ... the *leg*]*s* of the king on *my* neck were thrown, my midst *and* [...]
29 [... ...] of my midst, they come against me at the *towe*[*rs* ...]’
30 [... ...] his pasture, the word of mouth [...]
31 ‘[... ...] in your palace you [...]
32 [... ...] upon/against [...]’
Lacuna

ii

Lacuna
1–4 Too broken for translation

5 [... ...] palace [... ...]
6 [... ...] your [... ...]
7 [... ...] ... with the launderer I/he/they speak(s) [... ...]
8 [... ...] Karandan-[... ...]
9a [... ...] my face
9b When/as with [... ...]

i 28 See the commentary to i 11.

ti-ik-ki(! tablet:DI)-*i*(?): For -*ia* becoming -*i* in Late Babylonian see Lambert, Or.n.s. 40 (1971) p. 95:26.

i 30–2 The speech of the official mentioned in i 20 may end with i 29 and i 31 may be spoken by the same person who was talking in i 13–19.

ii 8 ^{kur}*Kár-an-da-an-*: This is otherwise unknown (it is not an attested orthography for Kar(an)duniaš).

10 [... ... *i*]*b-bal-kit* ^{lú}*rabûti*^{meš} *un-de-*[... ...]
11 [... ...] zi/nam *qaq-qa-ri uk-da-na-ta-*[... ...]
12 [... ...]-*ú na-áš-qu-ú šēpē*^{II}-*k*[*a*(?) ... ...]
13 [... ...]*il-tak-nu-ma ga-*TUK*-ru-tú-uk be-li lu-*[... ...]

14 x x x x [*i*(?)-*š*]*á-as-su-ú adi lìb-*⌜*bi*⌝ *ekalli* [... ...]
15 *ana ekalli*![*i šu*(?)-*r*]*i*(?)-*ba-in-nu* ^{lú}*rabûti*^{meš} *banû*(dù)^{ú} *Bābìli*^{ki} *lu-*[...]
16 *a-na* ^{d}*Bēl bēl* [*bēlē*^{meš}] *lu-ṣal-la šá a-da-nu-ú-a la ú-maš-*[*ši* ...]
17 *a-da-nu-ú-a* [*ú-š*]*e-eṣ-ṣa-an-ni a-da-an-nu-ú-a ú-še-reb-*[*an*(?)-*ni* ...]
18 *a-da-nu-ú-a* [*ú*]-*še-zi-za-an-ni ina puḫri šá* ^{lú}*ummāni*^{m}⌜^{eš} ...]

19 *la ta-pal-là*[*ḫ*] *šàr bēlē*^{meš}-*ni banû*(dù)^{ú} *Bābìli*^{ki} *ta-*[...]
20 *a-na* ^{d}*Bēl bēl b*[*ēlē*]^{meš} *tu-ṣal-la šá a-da-nu-ka la ú-maš-ši* x [...]

21 *a-da-nu-ka* [*ú*]-*še-ṣu-ka a-da-nu-ka ú-še-r*[*e-bu*(?)-*ka* ...]

22 x [x] x ŠU^{II} [*i-r*]*u-ub a-na É-sag-íl iš-kun pā*[*nē-šu* ...]
23 [... ...] x *ú-na-aš-šaq šá pa-paḫ* ^{giš}*dalāti*^{me}[^{š} ...]
24 [... ...]-*šú a-na* ^{d}*Bēl il-la-ku-' su-p*[*u-ú-šú* (...)]

ii 10 See the note to i 7.

ii 11 Cf. iii 32. The only root that seems at all appropriate is *katāmu*, *uk-da-na-ta-*[*am*/*mu*].

ii 13 W.G. Lambert suggests: *ga-ši*(! text:TUK)-*ru-tú uk-tel-li-lu*.

ii 15 Cf. ii 19. ^{lú}*rabûti*^{meš} *banû*(dù)^{ú} *Bābìli*^{ki}; *bēlē*^{meš}-*ni banû*(dù)^{ú} *Bābìli*^{ki}; and *ba-nu-ti-'* iii 7: Evidence for a Middle Babylonian term *banû* (written syllabically and ^{lú}DÙ) 'noble' has been summarized by von Soden, AHW p. 102a. In CAD 2 (B) p. 95 this meaning has not been accepted and the Middle Babylonian examples are interpreted as *bānû* 'housebuilder.' (In CAD ibid. one Middle Babylonian reference to ^{lú}ŠIDIM – PBS 2/2, 73:26 – is cited.) There is evidence, however, in favour of a Middle Babylonian word *banû* 'noble.' The references in this epic can hardly be to 'housebuilders.' Moreover, in a late copy of a MB letter (AfO 10 [1935–6] pp. 2–3 and see Grayson, Assyrian Royal Inscriptions 1 [Wiesbaden 1972] §§ 937–8) both the word *banû* 'to act as a noble' (cf. CAD 2 [B] p. 92a) and the word *būnu* 'nobility(?)' (cf. CAD 2 [B] p. 322a) appear. In Neo-Babylonian, *banû* 'noble' is replaced by *mār banî* (see

10 [... ... he] *rebelled*, the officers I/he/they [... ...]
11 [... ...] ... ground, I/he/they constantly *cov*[*er* ... ...]
12 [... ...] ... they are kissing *yo*[*ur*] feet [... ...]
13 [... ...] they established and your ... , my lord, may I/he/they [... ...]'
14 ... *they* (will) shout into the palace [... ...]
15 '[*Take*] me *in*to the palace, O officers, O nobles of Babylon, that I might [...]
16 To Bel, lord of [lords], let me pray that me alone he might not for[get ...]
17 That me alone [he] might bring me out, me alone he might bring [me] in [...]
18 That me alone [he] might cause me to stand in the assembly of the people [...]'
19 'Do not fear, O king, our lords the nobles of Babylon you [...]
20 To Bel, lord of l[ords], you may pray that you alone he might not forget [...]
21 That you alone [he] might bring you out, you alone he might bring [you in ...]'
22 ... hand [he] entered Esagil, he headed to[ward ...]
23 [... ...] he kisses, the doors of the shrine [...]
24 [...] his [...] to Bel go [his] prayer[s (...)]

von Soden, AHW p. 102a and pp. 615–16). As indicated by ii 19 the official ^{lú}GAL.DÙ (the plural of which is, in any case, ^{lú}GAL.DÙ^{meš}) (see the commentary to i 20) is not involved here.

ii 16 *a-da-nu-ú-a*: Cf. ii 17–18 and 20–1. This appears to be an otherwise unattested form of *ēdēnu* (see CAD and AHW s.v.). There is no phonetic objection to such an interpretation and the word does make sense here. *adannu* 'deadline' is improbable.

ii 17 Cf. ii 21. *aṣû u erēbu* 'to go in and out, to move freely.' See CAD 4 (E) p. 263 and AHW p. 235. In ii 21 [*ú*]-*še-ṣu-ka* is clearly subjunctive and therefore ii 17f. and 21 must be governed by the *šá* in ii 16 and 20 respectively.

ii 19 See the commentary to ii 15.

ii 22 Cf. iii 26, 31.

ii 24 For the restoration see BM 34113 (chapter 8): 18 and the commentary to that line.

25 [... ...] ^{d}*Bēl ilāni*^{meš} *mātāti*(kur.kur)^{meš} *i-ta*(?)-*mar-*'
qa-l[*a-* ...]
26 [... ...*ḫi*]-*ṭa-tu-šú gíl-la-tu-šú ú-ba-as-sa*[*r* ...]
27 [... ...]-*tu-šú i-da-am-mu-ú* ^{lú}ERÍN *ki-din-*[*ni* ...]

28 [... ...*É-sa*]*g-gíl i-dal-lal da-li-*[*lu* ...]
29 [... *a-n*]*a* ^{d}*Marduk it-ta-qa nīqē*(siskur$_{x}$) [...]
30 [*e-li*(?) ...] x x x *u*(?) ^{d}*É-a i-ṭeb-bu-*[*ú*(?) ...]
31 [... ...] x x x x x x x x [...]
Lacuna

iii

Lacuna
1 [x g]a(?) a k[a(?) ... ...]
2 [x]-ú *a-pi-i* x [... ...]
3 [x] *dul-lu g*[*u*(?)- ... ...]
4 x *u* [x] x x [x] x x [... ...]
5 [*l*]*u-lim ṣa-ri-ri ḫurāṣi* in za(?) [... ...]
6 [x]-*tu a-a* ' ma ^{d}*Nusku m*[*i*(?)- ... ...]
7 *id-du-uk ba-nu-ti-' ár-ḫ*[*iš* ... ...]
8 [^{m}]*Re-mut* ^{m}*Šàr-ilu-ú-a e-ru-*[*bu*(?) ... ...]
9 [*k*]*aspa a-na nak-k*[*am*]-*du ekalli*^{l}[^{i} ... ...]

ii 25–31 There are a few features of this passage which are reminiscent of the passage regarding the king in the Akītu ritual. Note the confession of sins in ii 26 and cf. F. Thureau-Dangin, Rituels accadiens (Paris 1921) p. 144:423; ^{lú}ERÍN *ki-din-*[*ni*] in ii 27 and cf. ibid. p. 144:426. In ii 25 should one restore *qa-l*[*a-al-šu*] in comparison with ibid. p. 144:427?

ii 27 *i-da-am-mu-ú*: For *idammumū*? Cf. *šu-ú*, a Late Babylonian variant of *šu-mi*, in Lambert, BWL p. 40:30 and see p. 290.

ii 30 Or *i-dab-bu-*[*ub* ...] 'he speaks.'

iii 5 Cf. iii 16. At the end perhaps restore *in-ṣa*(?)-[*abtu* '(ear)ring' or *in-za*(?)-[*hurētu* 'red-dyed wool.'

iii 6 Cf. iv 6.

iii 7 See the note to ii 15.

25 [… …] Bel, gods of the lands, *saw* … […]

26 [… …] his misdeeds (and) his crimes, he praises […]
27 [… …] his … was *moaning*, the people under divine protect[ion …]
28 [… … Esa]gil he praises […]
29 […] to Marduk he made sacrifices […]
30 [*to the gods* …] … *and* Ea they are pleasing […]
31 [… …] … … […]
Lacuna

iii

Lacuna
1–4 Too broken for translation

5 A deer of reddish gold … [… …]
6 … … Nusku … [… …]
7 He killed the nobles, quickly [… …]
8 Remut (and) Shar-ilua *ent[ered* … …]
9 Silver to the palace treasury [… … *they donated*].

iii 8 What appear to be traces of the beginning of this line (see copy) are probably traces from column iv.

Re-mut: He may be identical with the man of the same name who is known, from a *kudurru*, to have lived at the same time as Adad-shuma-usur (see L.W. King, Babylonian Boundary-Stones [London 1912] no. 3 iii 11, 27, 31).

^{m}*Šàr-ilu-ú-a*: The same name appears in J.N. Strassmaier, Babylonische Texte, Heft VI (Leipzig 1889), Inschriften von Nabuchodnosor 419:1 and ibid., Heft III (Leipzig 1888), Inschriften von Nabonidus 764:4; cf. K.L. Tallqvist, Neubabylonisches Namenbuch, Acta Societatis Scientiarum Fennicae 32/2 (Helsinki 1902) p. 201. Note the Assyrian name *Šar-illiia* in K.L. Tallqvist, Assyrian Personal Names, Acta Societatis Scientiarum Fennicae 43/1 (Helsinki 1914) p. 217, which is probably an abbreviation of *Šar-ilāni-iliia* (see ibid. p. 216 for references). No examples of this name appear in A.T. Clay, Personal Names from Cuneiform Inscriptions of the Cassite Period, Yale Oriental Series, Researches 1 (New Haven 1912).

10 [*i*]*l*(?)-'-*su nap-ḫa*[*r*] ^{lú}*um-man-nu šá*-[*nin*(?) ……] x x [x] x x […]

11 [*l*]*i-tab-nu-*' ^{giš}*nalbatta*(⸢ù⸣.šub.ba) ⸢*a*⸣-[*gur-ru* …] x ṣe ni/ir […]

12 [*lu-u*]*š-dan-*⟨*na-an*⟩ du$_8$ ṭu [pa š]ú *sa-ma-a-tú* [*dūri* … *l*]*i-li*-[…]

13 […… ^{gi}]^{š}*dalāti*^{meš} *dūri a*[*bullāti*^{meš} *dūri*(?)] lu gaz […]

14 […] ⸢*e*(?)⸣-*pu-uš ul t*[*a* ……] ḫi du x […]

15 [x] x x [x x] x a *e-te-pu-u*[*š* …] x […]

16 [*l*]*u-lim ṣa-ri-ri ḫurāṣi a-na makkūr* ⸢*É*⸣- [……] x […]

17 ^{na_4}*unqu*(šu.gur) *sal-te ekurri* [……]

18 *al-si* ⸢*nap*⸣-*ḫar* [^{l}]^{ú}*um-man-nu šá-nin* šu(?) [……]

19 *kīma kakkabāni šá-ma-a-*⟨*me*⟩ [*i*]*t-ta-na-an-bi-ṭu* [……]

20 *al-sa* ^{lú}*ḫa-za-*⸢*an*⸣-*ni Bābili*^{ki} ^{lú}*rubê*^{meš} *šá* [……]

21 *il-tab-nu-ú* ^{giš}*nalbatta*(⸢ù⸣.šub.ba) *a-gur-ru šá sa*-[*ma-a-tú*(?) ……]

22 ⸢*uš*⸣-*dan-na-an* du [ṭ]u pa šú *sa-ma-a-tú dūri* [……]

23 *az-qu-u*[*p* ^{gi}]^{š}*d*[*alāti*^{meš}] *dūri abullāti*^{meš} [*dūri*(?) lu gaz ...]

24 *a-di* LUGAL zi […] x *lu-ú* x [……]

25 *a-na Im-gur*-⸢^{d}⸣[*En-líl* x] x ta(?) x [……]

26 *šarru ana Bar-sìp*^{ki} *iš-šak-k*[*a-nu pānūšu*] *i-ru-u*[*b ana Ezida*(?) …]

27 *aḫ-ta-ṭa-a-ku bēl* [*bēlē*(?)]^{meš} *ḫi-ṭu-ú* [……]

iii 10 Cf. iii 18. [*i*]*l*(?)-'-*su* is an error for [*i*]*l*(?)-*su*-'. It is possible to read [*a*]*l*- rather than [*i*]*l*-.

iii 11–13 Cf. iii 21–3.

iii 12 And cf. iii 22: This is the first example of a ŠD of *danānu*. Does du$_8$/du ṭu pa represent *gabadibbu*?

iii 16 Cf. iii 5.

iii 17 *sal-te*: Cf. [^{n}]^{a_4}KA *zaq-te sal-te* R.C. Thompson, Assyrian Medical Texts (London 1923) 101, 3:8 (see R.C. Thompson, A Dictionary of Assyrian Chemistry and Geology [Oxford 1936]pp. 83–4). For *salātu* 'to cut' see

10 *They* exhorted all the craftsmen, *a ri*[*val* ... ...] ... [...]

11 'Let them make with the brick-mould the baked b[ricks *of the crenels*] ... [...]
12 [Let him] strengthen *its parapets*, the crenels [of the wall ...] ... [...]
13 [... ...] the doors of the wall, the g[ates *of the wall*] ... [...]
14 [...] make, do not [... ...] ... [...]
15 ... [...] ... *keep* making [...] ... [...]
16 A deer of reddish gold to the property of E[sagil/the t[emple ... ...] ... [...]
17 A stone seal, *carved*, of Ekur/the temple [... ...]'
18 'I exhorted all the craftsmen, a rival [... ...]
19 "Like the stars of heaven they will constantly shine [... ...]"
20 I exhorted the mayor of Babylon, the princes of [... ...]
21 They made with the brick-mould the baked bricks of the *cr*[*enels* ... ...]
22 I strengthen its parapets, the crenels of the wall [... ...]
23 I installed the d[oors] of the wall, the gates *of* [*the wall* ... ...]'
24 Until/towards the king [...] ... [... ...]
25 To Imgur-[Enlil] ... [... ...]
26 The king hea[ds] towards Borsippa, he entere[d *Ezida* ...]

27 'I have continually sinned against you, O lord *of* [*lords*], sins [... ...]'

Weidner, American Journal of Semitic Languages and Literatures 38 (1921), p. 189; cf. Lambert, BWL p. 283 and von Soden, AHW p. 1014b and 1016b.

iii 18 Cf. iii 10.

iii 19 *šá-ma-a-*⟨*me*⟩: There is no room for *-me* in the break.

iii 21–3 Cf. iii 11–13.

iii 22 See the note to iii 12.

iii 27 *bēl* [*bēlē*(?)]^{meš}: Although in Borsippa, the title indicates that Marduk is being addressed.

28 *un-ṭi-ib zi-i-m*[*u*(?)] x *šub-tu-šú pa-paḫ šá* [… …]

29 *a-ra-aḫ ūma-a-tum šuma*(mu?) *iq-ta-bí as-kar-šú* x [… …]

30 *sūq*(sila) *āli tam-la-a ú-mál-la šá isinni rēšē*^{meš}*-šú ú-š*[*e*/*l*[*i*/*t*[*u*/*b*[*u-*
… …]

31 *šarru ultu Bar-sìp*^{ki} *ú-ṣa-am-mu ana Kutê*^{ki} *iš-kun* [*pānēšu* … …]

32 *i-ru-ub ana É-*[*mes-l*]*am ina qaq-qar uk-da-*⌜*na*⌝*-ta-*[… …]

33 [… …] EN *Kutê*^{ki} [… …]

34 [… … *tukul*(?)]*-ta*(?)*-ka*(?) ^{d}*Nergal*(u.g[ur]) [… …]

Lacuna

iv

Lacuna

1 [… …] x [… …]

2 [… …] x x [… *i*]*š*(?)*-kun*(?) x [… …]

3 [… …] x […] x [… …]

4 [… …] x [x] uš(?) […] x [… …]

5 [… …] x x x ṭu(?) […] x [… …]

6 [… *k*]*u*(?)-' *ana* ^{d}*Nusku mi-*x […] x a(?) [… …]

7 […] x-*tu-' adi da-ba-b*[*u* … …]

8 […] x x-*šú*(?) ^{lú}*ikkaru* ka x […] x x x x [… …]

9 [… ^{l}]^{ú}*paḫāru*(báḫa[r]) iš(?) pur(?) ru(?) *a-n*[*a*(?)] x^{meš}
qur-qu x […]

10 […] x ú x x x tú *ana pāni* ^{SAL}*Su-ḫa-'-i-tum* ḫu/gi/zi […]

11a [… …]*-ú-tú* x [x] x

11b *a-na* ^{lú}*ašlāki*(azalag) gal ka x […]

12 […] ^{lú} *paḫāru*(báḫar) x [x x x k]a *su-ur-ru* EN BE […]

13 […] LUGAL x [… …] x ma nu x [x]

iii 28 *un-ṭi-ib*: The only root that makes sense is *ṭubbu* (*ṭâbu*) although no example with *zīmū* is given in CAD. Can *unṭîb* develop from *uṭṭîb* on analogy with the forms discussed by von Soden, GAG § 32b and Aro, Studia Orientalia 20 (1955) pp. 35–7?

iii 29 Or *a-ra-aḫ ūma-a-tum-mu iq-ta-bí* 'for a full month he spoke.'

28 *He made glad his* face, his dwelling, the shrine of [... ...]
29 A full month, the name he spoke, his crescent [... ...]
30 He builds up the city street(s) with fill, the beginning of the festival he [... ...]
31 The king came out of Borsippa and hea[ded] toward Cuthah [... ...]
32 He entered E[mesl]am, in/with the ground he constantly *cov[ers* ... ...]
33 [... ...] ... Cuthah [... ...]
34 '[... ...] *your* [*help*], O Nergal, [... ...]'

Lacuna

iv

Lacuna

1 [... ...] ... [... ...]
2 [... ...] ... [... *he*] *established* [... ...]
3–5 Too broken for translation

6 [...] to Nusku ... [...] ... [... ...]
7 [...] ... until/so long as speaking [... ...]
8 [...] *his* ... the farmer ... [...] ... [... ...]
9 [...] the potter ... *t[o]*...s, ... [...]

10 [...] ... ... before the Suhaean woman ... [...]
11a [... ...] ... ...
11b to the launderer ... [...]
12 [...] the potter [...] ... ... [...]
13 [...] the king [... ...] ... [...]

iii 30 Note that Nebuchadnezzar II used fill (*tamlû*) in building the processional streets of Babylon (see Langdon, VAB 4, p. 136 vii 53 and p. 160 A vii 51).

iii 32 See the commentary to ii 11.

iv 6 Or ^{md}*Nusku-mi*-x. Cf. iii 6.

iv 10 ^{SAL}*Su-ḫa-'-i-tum*: Cf. iv 18 and chapter 5, n.6.

14 [... ...] x *it-ta-din na-gi-tú ekalli-šú-*[*ma*(?)]
15 [... ... *ultu*] x-*ri* ^{uru}*Ḫu-da-da adi sa-pan-na* DIŠ DIN(?)
16 [... ...] *É-sag-gíl* IṢ BAT *it-ta-din Dūr-an-ki ki-ṣir* [...]

17 [... ...]-*a it-ta-din* ^{uru}*bir-tú šá-na-an ma-a-tú aḫi*(?) *šarri ú-pe*(?)-*ti*(?)
18 [... ...]-*bur*(?) ^{lú}*Su-ḫa-' ina naspante*(iš)^{te} *šāri ālāni*^{meš} *u appārū*^{meš}
19 [... ...] x *ib-bu-du it-ta-din a-na* ^{lú}*tar-din-nu ba*(?)-*ab* x iḫ(?) x
20 [... ... *i*]*t-ta-din ma-ad-bar-šú šá* ^{uru}*Ḫu-da-*⸢*da*⸣
21 [... ...] x šá(?) kur *ana šadî*^{i} *šá Ḫa-ši-mur mi-ṣir* [$^{\text{íd(?)}}$*Za*(?)-*a*]*b-bi elî*(an)^{i}
22 [... ... *i*]*l-tak-nu-' āla ina rēši-šú*
23 [... ...] x-*šú ši-i am- rat-su* [Ḫ]AR-*tum*
24 [... ...]-*ú-tú u* x kur ab
25 [... ... LU]GAL(?) EN-*šú ta-kar-rab*
26 [... ...] x ku *bil-tú*
27 [... ...] KÁ-*ka*
28 [... ...] x [x] *pa-na e-pu-šú*
29 [... ...] *appārū*^{meš}
30 [... ...] x^{meš}-*šú*
31 [... ...] x
32 [... ...] x

Lacuna

iv 15 DIŠ DIN(?): Should one read *ana-din* 'I shall give'?

iv 16 IṢ BAT: Read either *iṣ-bat* or *iz-ziz*.

iv 19 *tardinnu*: See Lambert, BWL p. 308 and Wilhelm UF 2 (1970) pp. 277–82.

iv 20 ^{uru}*Ḫu-da-*⸢*da*⸣: There is probably nothing missing in the break between *da* and ⸢*da*⸣.

14 [... ...] he gave, the *district* of his palace [*and*]
15 [... ... from] ... Hudada to the plain ...
16 [... ...] Esagil he seized/stood, he gave, Duranki the band of [...]
17 [... ...] he gave, fortress, ...

18 [... ...] the Suhaean(s), with the destruction of wind, cities and marshes
19 [... ...] ..., he gave, to the second son ... ...
20 [... ... he] gave, the desert of Hudada
21 [... ...] ... to the mountain of Hashimur, border of the *Upper* [*Za*]*b*
22 [... ...] they established the city at its top.
23 [... ...] that [...] of his, his inspection ...
24 [... ...] ... and ...
25 [... ... the *ki*]*ng* his lord you will bless
26 [... ...] ... tribute
27 [... ...] your gate
28 [... ...] ... [*which*] previously he had made
29 [... ...] marshes
30 [... ...] his [...]s
31–32 Too broken for translation

Lacuna

iv 21 *mi-ṣir* [$^{\text{id}(?)}$*Za*(?)-*a*]*b-bi elî*(an)^{i}: The reading is reasonably certain but the text is probably corrupt. In an inscription of Shalmaneser III (Die Welt des Orients 2 [1954–9] p. 154:110–11) Ḫašimur is mentioned in connection with the Lower Zab! Further comment on Ḫašimur will be found in Brinkman, PKB p. 156, n. 941. For *miṣru* with canals see von Soden, AHW s.v.

iv 22 *rēši-šú*: The *šú* is a peculiar form but the reading seems appropriate.

7

Nabopolassar Epic

Only one fragment (BM 34793 = SP II, 286 + 525) of the Nabopolassar epic has been preserved. This small piece is, however, of unusual significance for it provides the only evidence that such an epic existed and the only account in Akkadian of an actual coronation. The full extent of the epic is unknown but since the concern in column ii(?) is with the defeat of the Assyrians and column iii(?) contains the account of Nabopolassar's coronation, it is apparent that the entire composition was concerned with Nabopolassar and mainly with his early years when he rose to power. In other words the epic is a literary account of the foundation of the Chaldaean dynasty.

The coronation of Nabopolassar,[1] which is described in column iii(?), is the sole narrative preserved in cuneiform of the ritual attending the accession of a Mesopotamian king.[2] The only comparable account is the crowning of Marduk as king of the gods in Enuma Elish (Tablet IV) where the ceremony is much more elaborate. Details of coronation rites throughout the ancient Near East are sparse; only two brief descriptions are found in the Bible, one for the coronation of Solomon (1 Kings 1:32–49) and one for Joash (2 Kings 11:12–20). It is of special interest to compare the exclamation 'O lord, O king, may you live forever!' (iii[?] 17) to the similar outcry attested in the Biblical coronations (1 Kings 1:34 and 2 Kings 11:12): 'Long live the king!' One of the most significant details about the narrative in the Nabopolassar coronation is the prominent role of

1 The fact that Nabopolassar ascended the throne is laconically recorded in the Neo-Babylonian chronicle series (see Grayson, ABC Chronicle 2:14f).

2 The annual participation of the king in the Akītu ritual was not a once-for-all coronation. Regarding Assyrian practice see my comments in 'The Early Development of the Assyrian Monarchy' in UF 3 (1971) p. 319, n. 50 and regarding Babylonian practice see my 'Chronicles and the Akītu Festival' in Actes de la XVIIe rencontre assyriologique internationale (Brussels 1970) pp. 160–70. For a recent discussion of Mesopotamian and Israelite coronation procedures see H. Sauren, Orientalia Lovaniensia Periodica 2 (1971) pp. 5–12.

the various officials of Babylonia, particularly the 'officers of Akkad.' Their wish that the king might 'avenge Akkad' in iii(?) 21 is appropriate for Nabopolassar as the conqueror of Assyria but is also reminiscent of the statement by the gods in Enuma Elish IV 13 that Marduk was their 'avenger.'

A description of the content of what remains of column ii(?) is difficult, for the ends of the lines are not preserved and the context is not entirely clear. It appears that at least the beginning (1–7) of the preserved portion describes a religious ritual. The direct speech in lines 8 and 9 appears to be a boast by either the Assyrian commander who is mentioned later or by Nabopolassar. Lines 10 and 11 contain a description of the bloody scene in Cuthah brought about by a clash of arms between the Assyrians and Babylonians. No other record of this engagement is known. The Assyrian commander watched from the palace roof and finally exhorted the Babylonian king to spare his life (12–14). But the king issued the necessary order and the Assyrian was slain (15–16). Just before the text of this column breaks off Nabopolassar is mentioned by name and reference is made to the goods of the Assyrian.

The first intelligible lines in column iii(?) describe the assembly of princes and their prayers regarding the sovereignty. The simple statement that Bel (Marduk) gave the ruling power to Nabopolassar (name actually missing) follows (line 5) together with a statement (7–8) by Marduk that he will conquer the king's enemies 'with the standard' and will place the king's throne in Babylon. Then (9–11) a courtier who holds the office of 'chair-bearer' conducts Nabopolassar to the throne while the standard is held over his head. He is presented with the royal seal (12). The officers of Akkad approach and pronounce blessings upon the king and express the wish that he will avenge Akkad (13–21).

The fragment may come from a tablet similar in size and shape to that on which the Adad-shuma-usur epic was written.[3] If so, this means the piece (c. 6 × 9.5 cm.) contains about one-sixth of the original text. The identification of obverse and reverse is by no means conclusive but the interpretation adopted here is the more probable. The copy has some Late Babylonian features.[4] Regarding scribal relations to other late copies of epic texts see chapter 4.

3 They are both written by a similar hand and they both have two columns on each side.

4 *-nu* for *-ni* in ii(?) 14; *iqeru* [*bu'*] for *iqru* [*bu'*] (see von Soden, GAG §18d) in iii(?) 14; aleph written at the end of plural verb forms in ii(?) 4, 15, 16, iii(?) 4, 15.

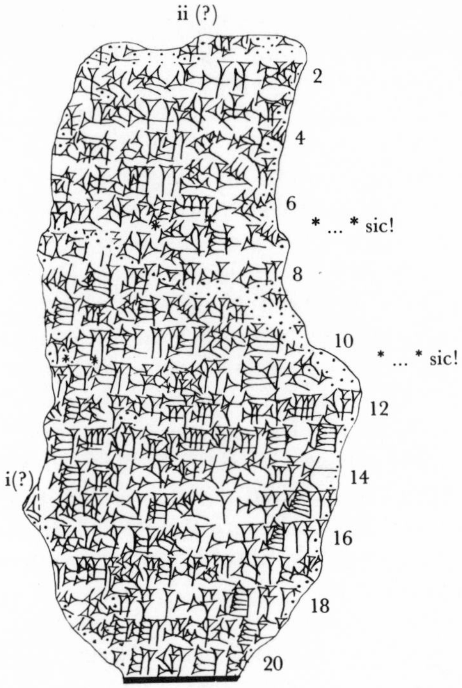

Obverse (?) of BM 34793 (SP II, 286 + 525)

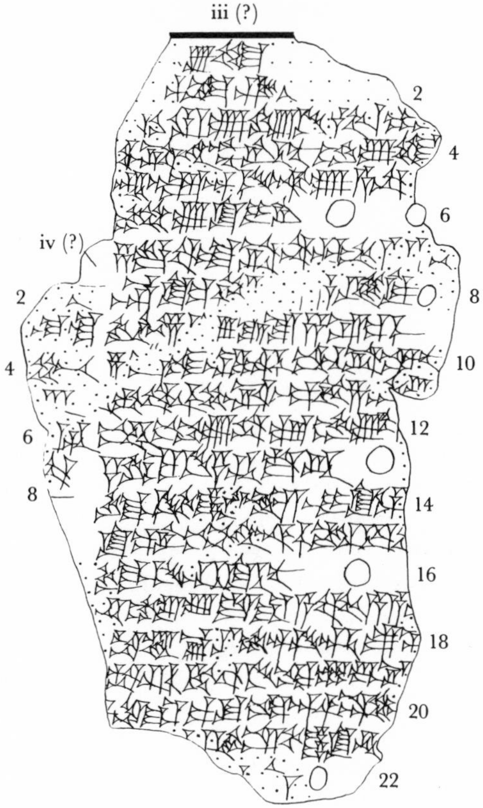

Reverse (?) of BM 34793 (Sp II, 286 + 525)

TRANSLITERATION

i (?)

Only traces are preserved. See the commentary.

ii (?)

Lacuna

1 [...] x x ru(?) x x x [......]
2 [*i-n*]*a šat mu-ši mašmašu* (maš.maš) *it-*[......]
3 [IZ]I(?) *zi-qa-a-tú ul-ta-*[......]
4 [*u*]*l-ta-ḫe-ṭu-' patrē*(gír)^{meš} [......]
5 *ultu ul-lu ana* ^{m}*Aḫḫē*^{meš}*-a* [......]
6 *e-ri pe-ṣu-ú aš-pu-*⌜*ú*(?)⌝ [......]
7 [*r*]*i-ba-a-tú ina abullāti*^{meš} x [......]
8 *man-nu kīma qarrādi* ^{d}*Nergal* [......]
9 *ad-duk* ^{lú}*rabûti*^{meš}*-šú ut-t*[*a*]-x [......]
10 *sūq* (sila) *āli ra-a*(! text:MIN)*-ṭu in-da-l*[*u* ......]
11 *nār*(?) ^{uru}*Kutê ina da-mu* x [......]
12 ^{lú}*ráb* ^{lú}*šá rēši dan-dan-nu ultu ú-ru* [......]

13 *šu-ú* ⟨⟨RU⟩⟩ *ultu ú-ru ekalli ki*[......]
14 *la ta-du-ka-nu šarra dan-nu* [......]
15 *li-du-ku-'* ^{m}*Aš-šur*^{ki}*-a-*[*a* ......]

16 *id-du-ku-'* ^{m}*Aš-šur*^{ki}*-a-*⌜*a*⌝ [......]
17 ^{md}*Nabû-ápla-uṣur šá ma-na-aḫ-tú ana pa-na* x [......]
18 [*b*]*u-še-e šá* ^{m}*Aš-šur*^{ki}*-a-*⌜*a*⌝ [......]
19 x x x ṣi ḫu du tú DUMU.U[Š(?) ......]
20 [x x] x x ru ma i[t ......]

It is reasonably certain that on the extreme left edge of the obverse(?) of this fragment traces of the ends of column i are preserved and that the beginnings of most lines in column ii are preserved. This much has been assumed in the transliteration and in the copy I have indicated the column division with a dotted line.

ii(?) 2 A reading [*qí-r*]*ib šat mu-ši* is not possible.

ii(?) 3 Cf. iii(?) 2. *zīqtu* and *zīqu* are otherwise attested only in Neo-Assyrian ritual and religious texts. See CAD 21 (Z), s.v.

ii(?) 6 *erû peṣû* is otherwise attested only once in OA and once in Sargon II (see AHW p. 857 sub *peṣû* 8c).

TRANSLATION

ii (?)

Lacuna

1 [...] ... ... [... ...]
2 [A]t night-time the *mašmašu*-priest [... ...]
3 [*Fir*]*e*, torches he/they ... [... ...]
4 They ... the daggers [... ...]
5 *From of old* to Ahheya [... ...]
6 'White' copper, jasper [... ...]
7 The squares at the gates ... [... ...]
8 'Who like the hero Nergal [... ...]?
9 I killed his nobles, I [... ...]'
10 The streets of the city, the drains, were filled [with blood ...]
11 The *canal* of Cuthah with blood ... [... ...]
12 The almighty chief eunuch from the roof [*of the palace looked down*],
13 When [*he saw* (*the scene*)] from the roof of the palace [he cried]:
14 'Do not kill me, strong king, [... ...]!'
15 (But the king commanded): 'Let the Assyrian be killed! [... ...]'
16 The Assyrian was killed [... ...]
17 Nabopolassar who the material before [... ...]
18 The possessions of the Assyrian [... ...]
19–20 Too broken for translation

ii(?) 8 Cf. the Adad-shuma-usur epic (chapter 6) i 10.

ii(?) 10 Cf. Era epic IV 34.

ii(?) 12 *dandannu*: This epithet is otherwise attested only with gods and Assyrian kings.

ii(?) 15 Cf. 16 and 18. *Aššurāiia* preceded by the personal name wedge is curious. Cf. the personal name $^{m(uru)}$ŠÀ.URU-*a-a* (references in Parpola, Neo-Assyrian Toponyms, AOAT 6 [1970] pp. 41–2).

iii (?)

1 [x x] iḫ(?) tu [... ...]
2 [x] x IZI *zi-q*[*a-a-tú*(?) ... ...]
3 [*p*]*aḫ-ru-ú* ^{lú}*rubû*^{meš} *šá māti* ^{md}*Nab*[*û-apla-uṣur* ...]

4 *pi-ta-' up-ni-šú-nu šarru-ú-tu* [...]

5 ^{d}*Bēl ina puḫur ilāni*^{meš} *palû*^{ú} *a-na* [...]
6 *šarru pu-ú ki-i-ni* [...]
7 *za-qip-tú at-ta-na-ak-šad a-a-b*[*i-ka*(?)]
8 *ina Bābili*^{ki} ^{giš}*kussâ*-[*ka*(?)] *a-nam-di*-[*i-ma*(?)]
9 ^{lú}*guzalû*(gu.za.l[á])^{ú} *qāt*^{II}-*su ṣa-bit* giš bar [...]
10 *za-qip-tum ina qaqqadi-šú il-ta-ka-nu*-['-*ma*(?)]
11 *ul-te-ši-bu-uš ina* ^{giš}*kussê šarru-ú*-[*tú* ...]
12 *il-qu-ú* $^{\text{na}_4}$*kunuk*(kišib) *šarru-ú-tú* [...]
13 *šá* ^{lú}*rēšī*^{meš} *šá ḫu-ṭa-ri* [...]
14 ^{lú}*rabûti*^{meš} ^{kur}*Akkadî*^{ki} *ina kúm-me i-qé-ru*-[*bu*-']
15 *ki is-ni-qu-' ina pāni-šú it-taš-b*[*u*-'-(*ma*)]
16 ^{lú}*rabûti*^{meš} *ina ḫu-di-šú-nu* [...]
17 *bēl šàr lu-ú da-ra-a-tú māt a-a-b*[*i* ...]

18 [*l*]*i-iḫ-dak-ka*(?) *šàr ilāni*^{meš} ^{d}*Márduk* URU ⌜E(?)⌝ [...]
19 [*l*]*i-ri-ik ūmē*^{meš}-*ka* ^{d}*Nabû tupšar*(sanga) *É*-[*sag-íl*]
20 ⌜^{d}⌝*Èr-ra* ^{giš}*kakka-ka* ^{d}*Nergal*(igi.du) *l*[*i*- ...]
21 [x (x)] x *gi-mil* ^{kur}*Akkadî*^{ki} EN [...]
22 [...] x x [...]

Lacuna

iii(?) 2 Cf. ii(?) 3.

iii(?) 4 *pi-ta-' up-ni-šú-nu*: This is an act of prayer. See von Soden, AHW p. 860a sub *petû* 16d.

iii(?) 6 *pû kîni*: Should this be connected with the *pû u lišānu* discussed by Oppenheim in History of Religions 5 (1965) pp. 250–65?

iii(?) 7 *at-ta-na-ak-šad*: Add this example to CAD 8 (K), sub *kašādu* 11 (p. 284a).

iii (?)

1 [...] ... [... ...]
2 [...] fire, *tor*[*ches* ... ...]
3 The princes of the land being assembled, Nab[opolassar *they bless*],
4 Opening their fists [they ...] the sovereignty.
5 Bel, in the assembly of the gods, [*gave*] the ruling-power to [*Nabopolassar*].
6 The king, the reliable command [...]
7 'With the standard I shall constantly conquer [*your*] enemies,
8 I shall place [*your*] throne in Babylon.'
9 The chair-bearer, taking his hand, ... [...]
10 They kept putting the standard on his head.
11 They had him sit on the royal throne [...]
12 They took the royal seal [...]
13 The eunuchs, the staff-bearers [...]
14 The officers of Akkad approached in the cella.
15 When they had drawn near, they sat down before him [(and)]
16 The officers in their joy [*exclaimed*]:
17 'O lord, O king, may you live forever! [May you conquer] the land of [your] enemies!
18 May the king of the gods, Marduk, rejoice in you ... [...]!
19 May Nabu, the scribe of E[sagil], make your days long!
20 May Erra, your sword, Nergal [...]!
21 [May you av]enge Akkad, ... [...]'
22 [...] ... [...]

Lacuna

iii(?) 8 After ^{giš}*kussâ* there is not room for *šarru-ú-tú.*

iii(?) 13 *šá ḫu-ṭa-ri*: Otherwise this official is attested only in Assyria.

iii(?) 19 *tupšar*(sanga) *É*-[*sag-íl*]: See Tallqvist, Studia Orientalia 7 (1938) pp. 102 and 381.

iii(?) 20 For ^{d}IGI.DU = Nergal in the Late Babylonian period see von Weiher, Nergal, AOAT 11 (1971) p. 93.

iv (?)

Lacuna

1 [......] x

2 [......]-*šú*(?)

3 [......]-*la*(?)-*la*

4 [......]-*bu-u*

5 [......] x

6 [......] x

7 [......]-*tú*

8 [......] x

Lacuna

(Too broken for translation)

8

Historical Epic Fragment regarding Evil-Merodach

This is a very small piece (BM 34113 = SP 213) of an historical epic. A coherent narrative is available only on the obverse where Nebuchadnezzar II (name partly restored) and Evil-Merodach are mentioned. If it is assumed that it came from the same kind of tablet as the Adad-shuma-usur epic then the obverse would be part of column i, which means that it is quite possible that the narrative came down as far as Nabonidus or even Cyrus. In the small portion that is preserved the main theme seems to be the improper behaviour of Evil-Merodach, particularly with regard to Esagil, followed by a sudden and unexplained change of heart and prayers to Marduk.

Only a description of the content of the obverse is possible and even here there are many uncertainties. In 2–4 Nebuchadnezzar is said not to have valued 'his' life and taken a good road somewhere. Then in 5–6 '*the* Babylon(*ian*)' speaks '*bad counsel*' to Evil-Merodach after which 'he gives an entirely different order.' In 7–14 someone, apparently Evil-Merodach (although the courtier in line 7 cannot be ruled out as a possibility), does not heed the advice but does various 'bad' things involving Esagil, Babylon, the cult-centres of the great gods, and neglect of son, daughter, family, and clan. Then suddenly he has a change of heart and in 15–18 he is said to have gone into the Holy Gate, one of the gates of Babylon, to pray to Marduk. At this point the narrative breaks off.

It is possible that this fragment comes from a tablet similar to that upon which the Adad-shuma-usur epic was written. Regarding scribal relations with other late copies of epic texts see chapter 4. If it does come from a tablet of similar size, the fragment would represent less than one-sixth of the original text and contain portions of columns i and iv. The piece measures c. 6 x 8 cm.

TRANSLITERATION

Obverse

Lacuna

1 [x x x (x)] ši zi x [... ...]

2 [^{md}*Nabû*]-*kudurrī-uṣur iḫ-tas-sa-s*[*u* ... ...]

3 [*na*]-*piš-tuš la i-qé-er ma-ḫar*-[*šu*(?) ... ...]

4 [*iz*]-*zi-iz-ma ur-ḫu damiq*(sig$_5$)-*tú š*[*á*(?) ... ...]

5 ⌜*u*(?)⌝ *Bābìli*^{ki} *ana* ^{m}*Amīl-*^{d}*Márduk i-ta-ma-a la mil-k*[*a*(?) ...]

6 *uš-taš-ni-ma i-nam-din ur-tam šanītam*(man)-*ma* [...]

7 *la i-šem-ma-a zi-kir šaptē-šú man-za-az p*[*a-ni* ...]

8 *ú-nak-kìr-ma ul* GIB^{ik} *ma-ḫar* [...]

9 *áš-šú du-muq É-sag-gìl u Bābìli*^{ki} *u kun* [*išdēšunu*(?) ...]

10 *ma-ḫa-za ilāni*^{meš} *rabûti*^{meš} *iḫ-tas-sa-su* ZA-*ri*-[...]

11 *libbu-uš e-li māri u mārti la i-nam-d*[*i* ...]

12 te su *ki-im-tú u sa-la-tú la i-ba-áš*-[*ši* ...]

13 *ina lìb-bi-šú a-na mim-ma šum-šú šá du-uš-šu*-[*ú* ...]

14 *uznu*(geštu)^{II}-*uš-šú là šaknat*^{at} *ana šul-lum É-sag-gíl* ⌜*u*(?)⌝ [*Bābìli*^{ki}(?)]

obv. 2 *iḫ-tas-sa-s*[*u*: See the commentary to obv. 17.

obv. 3 *napištuš la īqer*: Cf. *napšātu ša* 2 *ṣābē ... ina pāni bēliia la iqqer* C.E. Keiser, Babylonian Inscriptions in the Collection of J.B. Nies 1 (New Haven 1917) 49:26–9 (Neo-Babylonian); *napištašu panuššu ul e*(var. *i*)-*qir-ma iḫšuḫa mītūtu* M. Streck, Assurbanipal, Vorderasiatische Bibliothek 7 (Leipzig 1916) p. 60 vii 32–3; *ša mītūtu iplaḫū napšatsun pānuššun te-qir-u-ma* ibid. p. 36 iv 56–7; *kīma uqnî napištī ina* IGI-*ka li-qir* L.W. King, Babylonian Magic and Sorcery (London 1896) 12:70; and cf. CAD 1/2 (A) pp. 205–6. Note in this example *ina pāni* has been replaced by *maḫar* as it has in obv. 8.

obv. 5 ⌜*u*(?)⌝*Bābìli*^{ki}: The *u* is reasonably certain. Less probable is a reading LÚ and, in any case, the usual orthography is ^{lú}DUMU E^{ki} = *mār Bābili*.

TRANSLATION

Obverse

Lacuna

1 [...] ... [... ...]
2 [Nebu]chadnezzar considered [... ...]
3 His life appeared of no value to [*him*, ...]
4 [H]e stood and [*took*] the good road *to* [...]
5 *And* (*the*) Babylon(*ian*) speaks *bad counsel* to Evil-Merodach [...]
6 Then he gives an entirely different order but [...]
7 He does not heed the word from his lips, the cour[tier(s) ...]
8 He changed but did not block [...]
9 Concerning the treasure of Esagil and Babylon and securing [*their foundations* ...]
10 The cult-centres of the great gods they/he considered ... [...]
11 He does not show love to son and daughter [...]
12 ... family and clan does not exist [...]
13 In his heart, towards everything that was abundant [...]
14 His attention was not directed towards promoting the welfare of Esagil [*and Babylon*].

obv. 6 Or translate 'Again he gives another order but [...]'

obv. 8 GIB^{ik}: Probably read *iprik*. Regarding *maḫar* for *ana/ina pāni* see the commentary to obv. 3.

obv. 10 *iḫ-tas-sa-su*: See the commentary to obv. 17.
ZA-*ri*-[...]: Both the words *ṣāriru*, a particularly precious gold, and *zarinnu*, a decorated stand for precious objects, come to mind.

obv. 11 Cf. *ilu lìb-ba lid-dak-ka* G. Contenau, Contrats et lettres d'Assyrie et de Babylonie, Musée du Louvre, Textes cunéiformes 9 (Paris 1926) 141:43 (Neo-Babylonian) and see AHW sub *libbu* A 7c (p. 550a).

15 *tu-ru-ṣa uznātu*(geštu)^{II}*-šú il-lik ina Bābi-el-l*[*i*(?) ...]
16 *ú-sap-pa-a bēl bēlī*(en.en) *iš-ši-m*[*a*(?) *qātēšu* (...)]

17 ⸢*i*⸣*-bak-ku ṣar-peš ana* ^{d}*Márduk ilāni*^{meš} *r*[*abûti*^{meš} ... ...]
18 [*i*]*l-la-ku su-pu-ú-šú e-l*[*i* ... ...]
Lacuna

Reverse

Lacuna
1 [...] x [... ...]
2 [...]*-ta-at-su* x [... ...]
3 [...] x mi il(?) x [... ...]
4 [...] tu un du ur x [... ...]
5 [...] x *ba-a-bu* ni e ḫi n[u(?) ... ...]
6 [...] x*-me-šú šu-qu-ur*(?) x [... ...]
7 [...] x bi a si im x [... ...]
8 [...]^{meš} *ul i-ta-ma* x [... ...]
9 [...] id x *ilāni*^{meš} x [... ...]
10 [...] *pa-la-a-ḫa ilāni*^{meš} [... ...]
11 [... ...] x *du-muq* x [... ...]
12 [... ...] x [... ...]
Lacuna

obv. 15 Cf. Lambert, BWL p. 34:80.
Bābi-el-l[*i*(?)]: On this gate see E. Unger, Babylon (2nd ed. Berlin 1970) pp. 201–6 and RLA 1, p. 366.

15 With his ears alert he went into the Holy Gate [...]
16 He prays to the lord of lords, he raised [his hands (in supplication) (...)]
17 He weeps bitterly to Marduk, the g[reat] gods [... ...]
18 His prayers go forth, to [... ...]
Lacuna

Reverse

Too broken for translation

obv. 17 *i-bak-ku*: The *-ū* is curious. Cf. *iḫ-tas-sa-su* in obv. 2 and 10. ^{d}*Márduk*: Or *ili-šú* '(to) his god.'

obv. 18 Cf. *a-na* ^{d}*Marduk bēl Bābili*^{ki} *il-la-ku su-pu-ú-*[*šu*] CT 13, 48:4 (epic of Nebuchadnezzar I). Also cf. Adad-shuma-usur epic (chapter 6) ii 24.

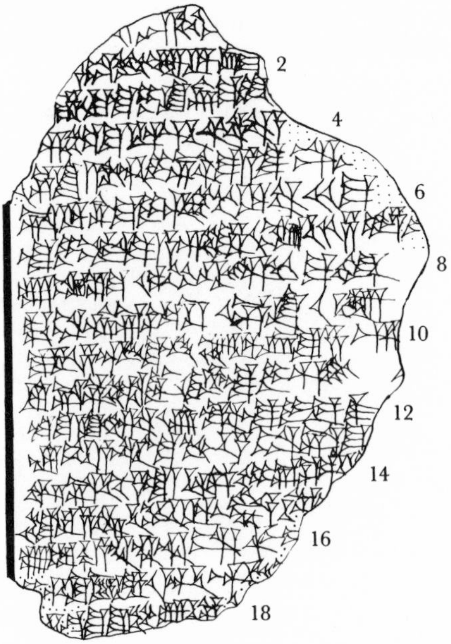

Obverse of BM 34113 (SP 213)

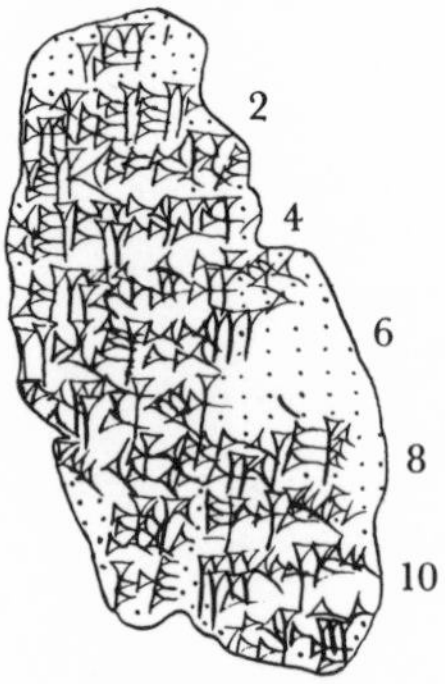

Reverse of BM 34113 (SP 213)

9

A Babylonian Historical Epic Fragment

The text preserved on this piece (BM 45684 = 81-7-6, 84) is so badly mutilated and poorly understood that it is impossible to date or place it with any confidence. Only one side, the reverse(?), is sufficiently coherent to warrant transliteration or translation and here there are only two suggestive clues as to the identity of the events narrated. These are the mention of a chief of the diviners called Salla and the concern with Cuthah, which possibly involved a battle between an enemy stationed there and the Babylonian king. But neither clue is very helpful. Since the personal name Salla does not seem to be attested before the Neo-Babylonian period this at least restricts the general time range.[1] The fact that a battle at Cuthah seems to be involved calls to mind the reference in the fragment of the Nabopolassar epic (chapter 7) to a Babylonian engagement with the Assyrians at the same city.[2] But beyond this it is impossible to go. Certainly there is no physical relation between the two fragments.

The obverse is too mutilated even to hazard a guess at its content. The first line of the reverse speaks of an arrival at Cuthah. Lines 2–6 introduce Salla, chief of the diviners, who consults the omens and predicts the happiness of the king and a defeat of the enemy by the camp of Akkad. After the speech of Salla the king moves quickly

1 The only other name of a chief diviner known is Aplāiia from the reign of Nebuchadnezzar II (see J.N. Strassmaier, Babylonische Text, Heft V [Leipzig 1889], Inscriften von Nabuchodonosor, no. 234:2–3). The name Ṣallā, written *Ṣa-al-la*, appears in ibid., Heft VII (Leipzig 1890), Inschriften von Cyrus, no. 169:5 and cf. *Ṣal-la-a-*AN ibid. no. 172:4. Since there are few Neo-Babylonian texts known before Nebuchadnezzar II the apparent absence of the name Ṣallā in Middle Babylonian onomastica merely suggests that the period concerned must fall some time during the entire Neo-Babylonian era.

2 Also note the references in both fragments to 'night-time' (*šāt mūši*).

(7–8). The remainder of the text (9–19) contains a first-person narration by the king. He describes his arrival at Cuthah at night and his greeting to someone. Then he seems concerned with the manner in which Cuthah is guarded by someone's son, and prays to Nergal. The text after this reference is in bad condition. It may have described a clash of arms with an enemy in Cuthah. If so, it is possible that r.(?) 1 refers to the arrival of this enemy at Cuthah.

Since this fragment was inscribed by a hand similar to the one which copied the Adad-shuma-usur epic (for full details of scribal relations of the late copies of historical epics see chapter 4), it may have come from a tablet of similar size and shape. If so, this fragment, which measures 9 x 6.5 cm., would represent less than one-sixth of the original text, but it is impossible to suggest which columns it would have contained.[3]

3 Note the late form *aq-ṭa-bi* in r.(?) 11 (see chapter 5, n. 8).

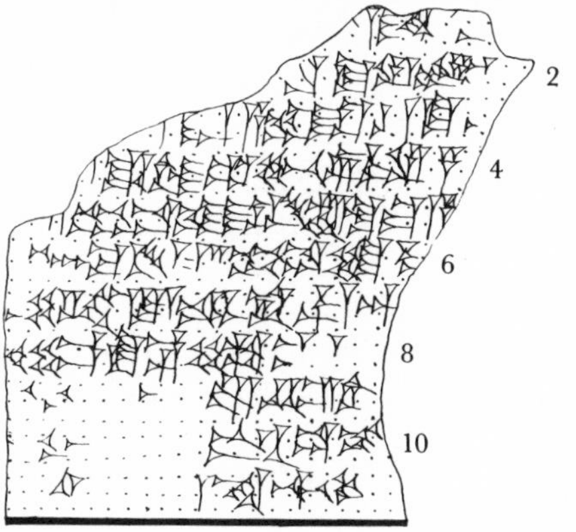

Obverse (?) of BM 45684 (81-7-6, 84)

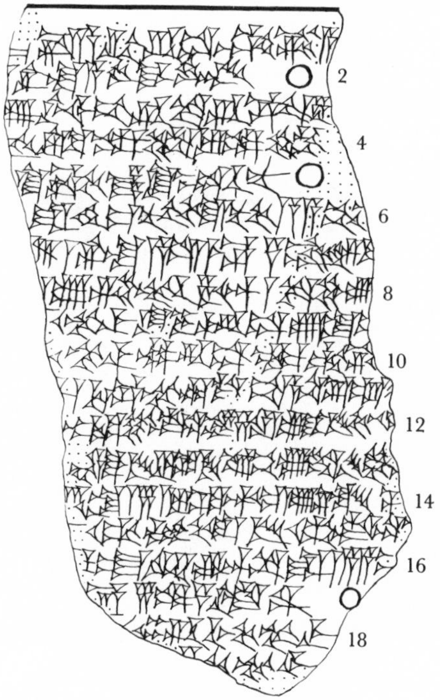

Reverse (?) of BM 45684 (81-7-6, 84)

TRANSLITERATION

Reverse (?)

1 [… …] x uš a *ik*(?)*-tal-du ina Kutê*[^{ki} … …]
2 [… …] ⌜^{m}⌝*Ṣal-la-a* ^{lú}*ráb* ^{lú}*bārî*(ḫal)^{meš} [… …]
3 [… …] *ú-šal-lim bi-ri te-re-e-tú ḫa-*[… …]
4 [… … *šà*]*r lìb-ba-ka li-ṭeb-ka li-*[… …]
5 [… …] *karāš* ^{kur}*Akkadî*^{ki} *dáb-du-šú-nu* [… …]
6 [… … *lu tu-/li* (?)]*-ra-ḫi-iṣ kul-lat-su-nu māt a-a-bi m*[*u*(?)*-* … …]

7 [… …] x ^{m}*Ṣal-la-a iš-me-e šá šarri im-m*[*a*(?)*-* … …]
8 [… …] x*-ú zi-mu-šú ḫa-an-ṭiš te-bu-ú* [… …]
9 [… … *ur-r*]*a*(?) *u mu-ši ki-i ar-du-ú at-t*[*a*(?)*-* … …]
10 [… … *ša*]*t*(?) *mu-ši ak-tal-du dūr Kut*[*ê*^{ki} … …]
11 [… …] x *šul-mu aq-ṭa-bi a-na É-mes-l*[*am* … …]
12a [… …] x *dūra in-da-na-aṣ-ṣa-ru-ú māra -šú*
12b kur be x [… …]
13a [… …] *abullāti*^{meš} *qarrādū*^{meš} *ina lìb-bi ú-šeš-šib*
13b ub x [… …]
14a [… … *ana*] *re-ṣi-iá ana qarrādi* ^{d}*Nergal ú-ṣal-la*
14b x [… …]
15 [… …] x *ul sisê*^{meš} *ul ina da-na-n*[*i*(?) … …]
16 [… …] x *at-tat-lak* ^{d}*Èr-ra ana a-a-bi* [… …]
17 [… …] KAL/DAG*-iá ka-šá-dam qa-*[*tu*(?) … …]
18 [… …] x mi ri šú *ina šat mu-ši* [… …]
19 [… …] x [*š*]*at mu-ši* [… …]
Lacuna

TRANSLATION

Reverse (?)

1 [......] ... they arrived in Cuthah [......]
2 [......] Salla, chief of the diviners, [......]
3 [......] he made complete, divination, omens, [......]
4 '[......] O king, may you be happy, may [......]
5 [......] the camp of Akkad, their defeat [......]
6 [...... May he/you] overwhelm all of them, the land of the enemy [......]'
7 [... the speech of] Salla he heard, [the ...] of the king ... [...]
8 [......] his face, getting up quickly [......]
9 '[...... *da*]*y* and night when I led/followed, *I/yo*[*u* ......]
10 [*When* ......] at night-[*tim*]*e* I arrived, the wall of Cuthah [......]
11 [......] I spoke greeting, to Emesl[am ......]
12a [......] *at* the wall whose son was keeping constant watch,
12b ... [......]
13a [......] the gates, warriors therein he stationed.
13b ... [......]
14a [...... to] help me I prayed to the warrior, Nergal,
14b ... [......]
15 [......] ... horses not in strengt[h ......]
16 [......] I had gone away, Erra to the enemy [......]
17 [......] my ... *ha*[*nd*] to capture [......]
18 [......] ... at night-time [......]
19 [......] night-time [......]'

Lacuna

PART III

10

Fragments

BM 34716 (SP II, 205)

It is not at all clear just what this broken inscription is. The fragment measures c. 12 x 7 cm. and, if the identification of obverse and reverse is correct, it comes from the lower left corner of a tablet of undetermined size. There was probably only one column on each side. A copy by T.G. Pinches has been published by C.B.F. Walker as CT 51, no. 74. The curious phrase in r.(?) 10 also appears in RM 742 (see below). The obverse(?) (see p. 104) is too broken to edit.

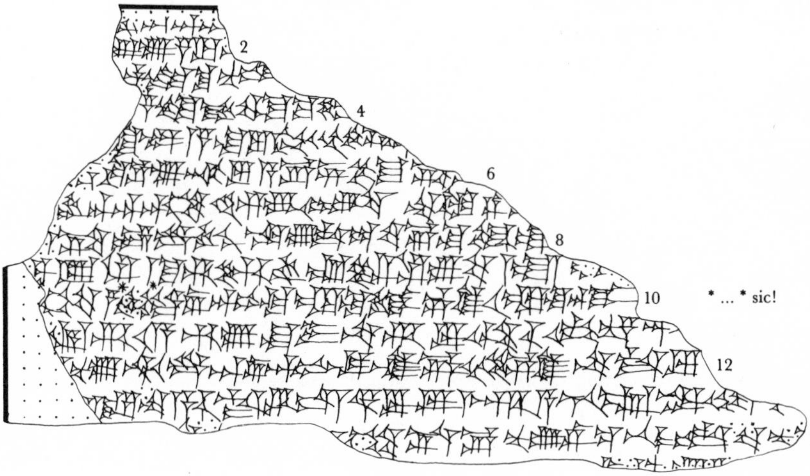

Reverse (?) of BM 34716 (SP II, 205)

TRANSLITERATION

Reverse (?)

1 [… … *š*]*àr ilāni*(dingir.dingir) ^{d}[*Marduk* … …]

2 [… …]-*ú ú-šá-lik* x [… …]

3 [… *ú*(?)-*na*]*p*(?)-*pil-šu-nu-tu*$_{4}$ [… …]

4 [… …] *šá tu-rap-pi-šu-ma l*[*i*- … …]

5 [… …] ki ka *ana šá-la-lu šal-lat Bābili*$^{⌜ki⌝}$ [… …]

6 […] x-*de-e ú-bal-lu a-dan-ni tu-ta*-x [… …]

7 […] *šàr ilāni*(dingir.dingir) ^{d}*Marduk im-šid mi-šit-tú ina ut-nin-ni* x [… …]

8 [*i*]*t-ta-as-kip* ^{lú}*nakir-ka ú-da-ap-par kal-la mur-ṣi* [*ina zumrika*(?) (…)]

9 [*i*]*l-ṭu-ru ana šu-ḫu-uz* ^{lú}*tup-šar-ru-ú-tam ana ṣi-i*[*ḫ*(?)-*rūti*(?) … …]

10 [^{d}]*Marduk šá ti*(?)-*kip sa-an-tak-ku al-la* ^{lú}*mār Bābìli*^{ki} *u al-la* $^{lú(!tablet: AN)}$*mār* [*Barsipa*^{ki}(?) … …]

11 [*šá*(?)] *nak-ri u a-ḫu-ú la i-na-ṭal-lu ši-pir-šú ul nu šá-an-n*[*i*(?) … …]

12 [x] x-*nu-ú ti-kip* ^{d}*sa-an-tak-ku ina qí-rib Bābìli*^{ki} *na-ṭa-lu* [… …]

13 […]x *šun-na-a-šú da-ri-iš šuk-lu-lu šip-ri a-ḫaz ṭuppi-ka u* x x [… …]

14 [… …] x x [*šàr ilāni*] $^{⌜d⌝}$*Marduk uš-tan-nu-ú-ni iṣ-bat pa-rik-te*(?) nu x [… …]

15 [… …] x x *ú* šá(?) [… …]

Lacuna

rev.(?) 3 f. There are traces of a line or gloss squeezed between these lines. All that remains is one small vertical above the ŠÁ in r.(?) 4.

TRANSLATION

Reverse (?)

1 [... ...] the king of the gods, [Marduk ... ...]
2 [... ...] caused to go [... ...]
3 [... *de*]*stroyed* them [... ...]
4 [... ...] which you spread [... ...]
5 [... ...] to plunder Babylon [... ...]
6 [...] ... they bring, (my) deadline you [... ...]
7 [...] the king of the gods, Marduk, paralysis seized, with prayers [... ...]
8 Your enemy has been overthrown, *all* sickness will be removed [*from your body* (...)]
9 They have written to teach the scribal craft to the *yo*[*ung* ... ...]

10 Marduk who the writing of cuneiform, the *corvée of* the Babylonians and the *corvée of* [the *Borsippeans* ... ...]
11 [*Who*] sees neither enemy nor foreigner, his work we cannot *chan*[*ge* ... ...]
12 ... the writing of cuneiform, within Babylon, to see [... ...]

13 [...] ... forever, to perfect skill, to learn your tablet, and ... [... ...]
14 [Which ... ...] ... [the king of the gods], Marduk, changed, he *opposed* ... [... ...]
15 Too broken for translation
Lacuna

rev.(?) 10 *ti*(?)-*kip*: There appears to be a TI written over an erasure.

rev.(?) 11 *i-na-ṭal-lu*: Cf. von Soden GAG §20g and Gelb BiOr 12 (1955), p. 101.

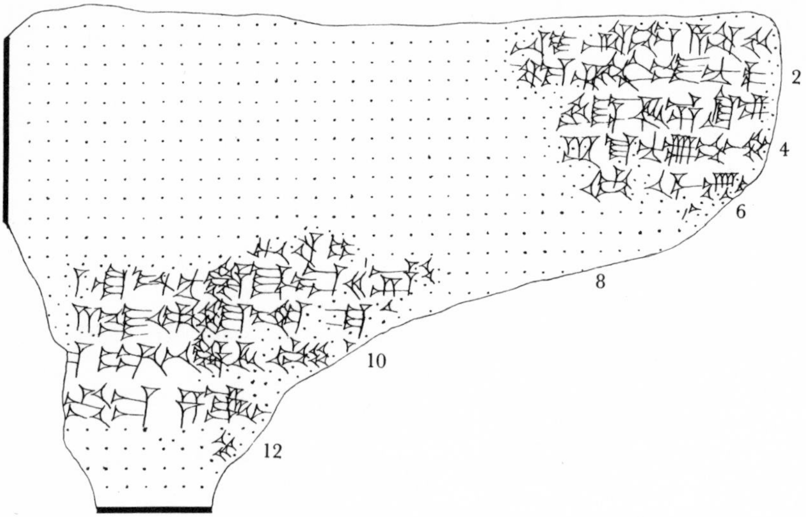

Obverse (?) of BM 34716 (SP II, 205)

RM 742

The identity of this fragmentary text is moot but it seems to have some connection with BM 34716 (see p. 101). It is a corner fragment which measures c. 4 x 5 cm.

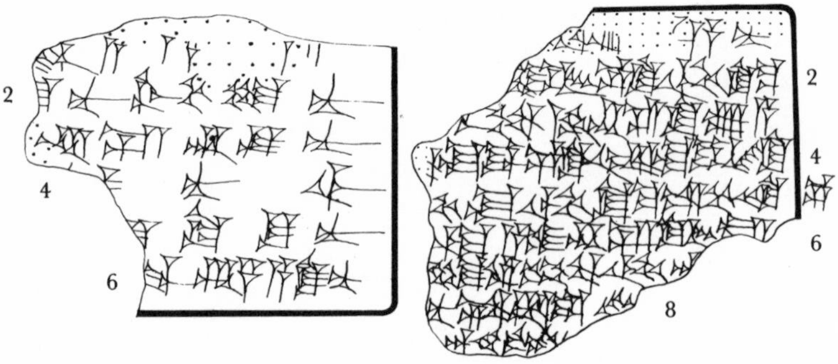

Side I (left) and side II (right) of RM 742

BM 36692 (80-6-17, 424)

The identity of this fragmentary text is unknown but the content obviously concerns the Isin II period. Note Nebuchadnezzar in r.(?) 10 and possibly Marduk-[kabit-aḫḫēšu] in obv. 6 and possibly Marduk-[nādin-aḫḫē] in r.(?) 11. Intriguing is the numeral following *a-di* 'until' in obv. 2. The figure is 30 + a number larger than 3. It may be mere coincidence but the number of years the statue of Marduk resided in Elam from the end of the Kassite Dynasty (c.1157 B.C.) to the reign of Nebuchadnezzar I (c.1126–1105 B.C.) could be 30 + a number larger than 1. Note the reference to Assyria – [^{kur}(?)*A*]*š*-*šur*^{ki} – in r. (?) 2. The fragment comes from the left edge and measures c. 6 × 2 cm.

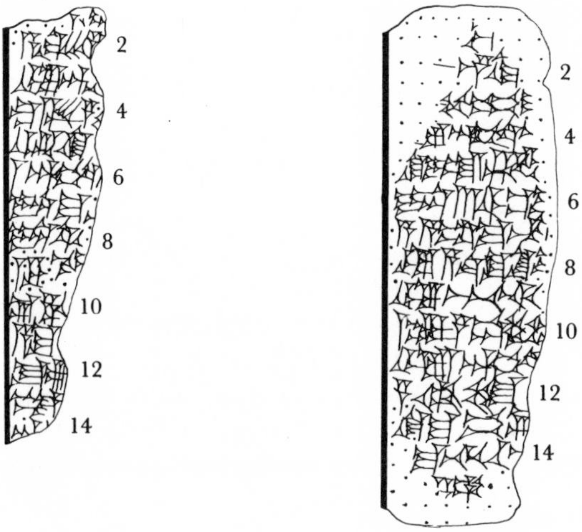

Obverse (?) (left) and reverse (?) (right) of BM 36692 (80-6-17, 424)

BM 35792 (SP III, 319)

This fragment contains narrative of an historical nature but it is impossible to say whether it belongs among chronographic or historical-literary texts. Note 'from the first to the seventeenth (day) people' ([*ul*]*tu* I *adi* ⸢XVII⸣ ^{lú}UN^{m}[^{eš} ... ...]); 'in fear and trepidation the land' (*ina ḫ̮at-tum u gi-lit-tum* KUR); 'descendant of Man*nu*[...' (*li-ib-li-ib-bu šá* ^{m}*Man-nu*(?)-[...); 'hostility was established' (*nu-kúr-tum iš-šak-nu*). It is a small fragment, measuring c. 3.5 × 5.5 cm., from the left edge of a large tablet inscribed in the slanting fashion characteristic of some tablets from the late period. Only one side and traces on the left edge have been preserved.

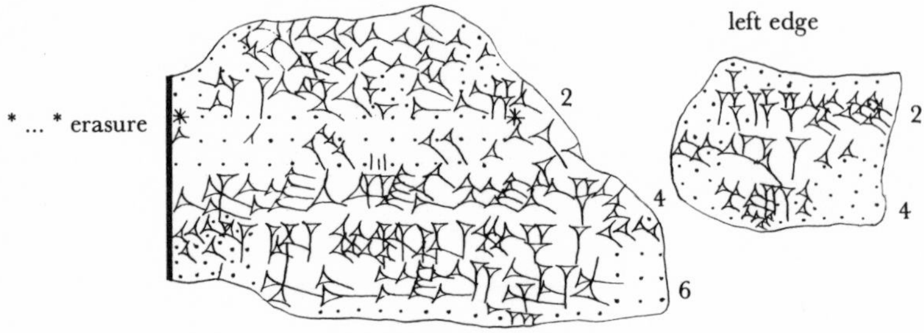

BM 35792 (SP III, 319)

BM 50857 (82-3-23,1851)

This appears to be a fragment of historical-literary material. Note 'king of the universe' (*šàr kiš-šá*(?)-*t*[*im*]) preceded by a name that seems to be Sargon (...]-*ki*(?)-*na* – the first sign is certainly not SUM). The references to sovereignty (6), throne (7), and oath-taking (*nap-ḫ̮ar-ši-na i-na ni-iš ilāni*^{me}[^{š} ... ... *m*]*a-mit ú-šá-aṣ-bit-su-nu-ti*) are particularly interesting. Also note the literary form *qer-bu-uš-un* (5). The fragment, of which only one side is preserved, measures c. 4 × 5 cm.

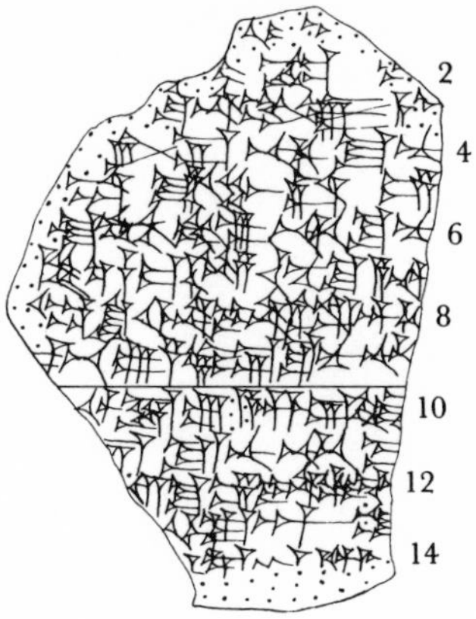

BM 50857 (82-3-23, 1851)

Indexes

MUSEUM NUMBERS

PUBLICATION REFERENCES OF HISTORICAL-LITERARY TEXTS DISCUSSED

AKKADIAN WORDS DISCUSSED

PROPER NAMES